"I absolutely loved *God in My Everythi*
meditation on living a fully, vibrantly
important for those starting their faith journey as for those far along the way. I highly recommend it for its real-world advice, poignant stories, and transformative prescription for a life of wholeness and joy."

Suzy Welch,
business columnist and author of
10–10–10: A Life Transforming Idea

"This is a book for the business executive, the mother of young children, the medical school student, the cat-in-the-hat madcap juggler of a thousand things. A must read for all busy people who have lost sight of Jesus and lost touch with themselves, and long to recover both. I need this book. My church needs this book."

Mark Buchanan,
pastor and author of
Your God Is Too Safe

"All who hunger for a life fully animated by the Holy Spirit will find themselves nourished by *God in My Everything*. Ken Shigematsu describes how he tapped into spiritual practices, both ancient and new, that feed his soul, and nurtured him toward becoming an energized and actualized disciple of Christ—and how we can do the same."

Tony Campolo,
Eastern University;
author of *Let Me Tell You a Story*

"In this thoughtful, holistic book, Ken winsomely invites us on a journey ... a journey that brings great hope, as we discover eyes to see and ears to hear that God is, in fact, present all around us."

Danae Yankoski,
coauthor with Francis Chan of
Crazy Love

"Ken Shigematsu really *gets* it. He gets how to actually enjoy the living God in every part of our lives and passes on practical, down-to-earth ways to help us develop our own unique 'rule,' enabling us to live an authentic friendship with Jesus Christ in our work, play, relationships, sleep—in our *everything*!"

Darrell W. Johnson,
First Baptist Church, Vancouver;
author, *Fifty-Seven Words That Change the World:
A Journey through the Lord's Prayer*

"This is the rare book birthed out of the crucible of outstanding pastoral leadership over many years. Filled with gems, insights, and hard-won lessons, I look forward to recommending *God in My Everything* to our leadership and entire church!"

Pete Scazzero,
pastor, bestselling author of
The Emotionally Healthy Church
and *Emotionally Healthy Spirituality*

"Ken leads us on a journey to a wide-open, spacious place, where we find spiritual refreshment and an invitation to enjoy God in a deeper way. For anyone stressed out, jaded, or even, dare I say it, bored in their faith, this book will be a source of great encouragement and inspiration."

Tim Hughes,
songwriter and director of worship at
Holy Trinity Brompton, London

KEN SHIGEMATSU

GOD
⤜ IN MY ⤛
EVERYTHING

How an Ancient Rhythm
Helps Busy People Enjoy God

ZONDERVAN®

ZONDERVAN.com/
AUTHORTRACKER
follow your favorite authors

ZONDERVAN

God in My Everything
Copyright © 2013 by Ken Shigematsu

This title is also available as a Zondervan ebook. Visit www.zondervan.com/ebooks.

Requests for information should be addressed to:

Zondervan, *Grand Rapids, Michigan 49530*

Library of Congress Cataloging-in-Publication Data

Shigematsu, Ken, 1966-
  God in my everything : how an ancient rhythm helps busy people enjoy God /
Ken Shigematsu.
    pages cm
  Includes bibliographical references.
  ISBN 978-0-310-49925-1 (pbk.)
    1. Spiritual life—Christianity. 2. Christian life. 3. Time management—Religious
aspects—Christianity. I. Title.
  BV4501.3.S5455 2013
  248.4'6—dc23   2013005448

Cover design: Ron Huizinga
Cover photograph: Masterfile
Interior design: David Conn

Printed in the United States of America

13 14 15 16 17 18 19 20 /DCI/ 20 19 18 17 16 15 14 13 12 11 10 9 8 7 6 5 4 3 2 1

To Sakiko, my best friend
and Joey, our beloved son
and to Tenth Church, our family in Christ

CONTENTS

FOREWORD

When an author claims to offer a framework for a life that is real—and truly worth living—one rightly wonders if what he writes is true in his own life. Rest assured: Ken Shigematsu "practices what he preaches."

I first met Ken when he was a student at Wheaton College. Then, while he was president of the student body at Gordon-Conwell Seminary, where I was a trustee, he drove me some distance to an appointment. On the way, I leaned back in my seat and asked him to tell me about his life. A bit reluctant to do so because of his Japanese-Canadian reserve, over the next hour he kindly unfolded his story. And I thought: this young man is real.

Later, he was part of our Arrow Leadership Program. I was immediately impressed with his knowledge but also with his humility. He was very bright and informed but had no need to show off. In the years since, Ken has become like a younger brother, almost a son to me. Through the ups and downs of ministry, the good times and hard ones, the testing and growing experiences of marriage, parenting, and leadership, I have sensed again and again: Ken is real. He now leads one of our mentoring groups of still-younger leaders, and I know each of them finds him the same.

I remember clearly a fall afternoon, years ago, when Ken came to Charlotte for a personal retreat. He shared with me the challenges he was facing as a young pastor and husband. As we sat on our patio in the afternoon sun, he read to me what he had written then about the way he wanted to live his life and serve the Lord.

Yes, what Ken writes here, honestly and helpfully, is already spelled out in his own life.

Not only so, but in writing about a "rule of life" he focuses not just about a slice of life—our spiritual practices—but about God in the whole of life—in play as well as in prayer, in body as well as spirit, with friends and family, in the use of money, at work and in worship.

A rule of life, as Ken describes it, is truly a way, or ways of life—of living out Jesus' first and great commandment: to love the Lord our God with all our soul, mind, heart, and strength—and his second: to love our neighbor as ourselves. He has taken the centuries-old practice of having a rule of life and translated it into the daily life of a modern follower of Christ—not just as a pastor but as an everyday Christian in the midst of a busy and very secular city.

So I heartily recommend this book to you, good reader, if you are seeking to be a real and authentic person.

St. Paul once wrote: "the reality is in Christ."

If you pay attention to what is here, I believe you will be drawn to a life that is in touch with reality, as you find a guide to help you journey with Christ in your everything.

Leighton Ford
Charlotte, North Carolina

PREFACE

When people hear I left a promising career at a Fortune 500 company in Tokyo and became an inner-city pastor in Vancouver, British Columbia, they express curiosity and at times astonishment. On the surface, these two vocations seem an ocean apart in more ways than one. But they are similar in this respect: they can both consume all of you.

When I worked in Tokyo I was considered a "7-Eleven" man— I'd leave my apartment at 7:00 a.m. and return from work after 11:00 p.m. When I began pastoring a declining, aging church in Vancouver, I rose early and worked late—frequenting the midnight Wendy's drive-through so often that the woman at the delivery window came to recognize my face and greet me by name. Whether I was ascending the rungs of a corporate ladder or fostering renewal and growth in an old, dwindling church, in all my busyness I felt like I was leading a shallow existence: spiritually treading water and squandering my relationship with God.

Perhaps you are neither a business person nor a pastor, but you find yourself consumed by your work, your studies, your family, your involvement in the church or community—all good things in and of themselves—but they feel like they're crowding out your life with God. In fleeting moments you yearn for a deeper, richer, more transforming friendship with God, but this seems elusive, perhaps even impossible. What if there was a way to experience God as your deep center, not only in your formal prayers and Bible reading, but in the *midst* of your studies, work, exercise, and play? What if there

11

was a way to enjoy God not only as you sit in quiet contemplation but as you move about your day? What if you could weave friendship with Christ into the fabric of everything you do without leaving your world and becoming a monk?

Several years ago, in an unexpected place, from an unlikely era in history, I discovered a rhythm that enables me to experience *God in my everything* without withdrawing from my current life.

Sometime later one of my colleagues was scheduled to preach at our church on a Sunday, but a family engagement unexpectedly came up and he asked me to fill in for him. I didn't have much time to prepare, so that Sunday I spoke extemporaneously about the rhythm of life I had been experimenting with, based on the teachings of ancient monks. The response was astounding, beyond anything I'd experienced in my fifteen years of pastoring at Tenth Church here in Vancouver. Over the next two months, a steady stream of people contacted me wanting to learn more.

A lawyer in our community, with whom I had never spent time, asked to meet for coffee. He told me he had listened to the recording of my sermon nine times and wanted to discuss how he could develop a rhythm for his own life. An artist from our church said with some irritation, "I don't believe in structure or schedules. They rub me the wrong way—but tell me more."

Since then I've done a lot of teaching on this theme of a rhythm of life, tapping into ancient wisdom for modern living and drawing on stories from my life as a business person, pastor, husband, and father. As I teach, I've found a great hunger among busy people from all walks of life to live with God less at the periphery and more at the core of their lives.

If you find yourself drawn to such a life, I invite you to take a walk down this ancient path that will set you free.

PART 1
RULES

— CHAPTER 1 —

MONKS, SAMURAI, AND THE CHRISTIAN LIFE

Several years ago my mentor, Leighton Ford, a seasoned Presbyterian minister, wrote to me and said he was organizing a ten-day pilgrimage to Ireland. The trip was originally for friends of his who were in their retirement years, but he hadn't been able to fill the tour quota for the travel agency so now he was inviting some of his younger friends.

I had never been to Ireland.

I had never been on a pilgrimage.

Thanks to an unexpected cash gift from my grandmother at just that time (she had offered to buy me a La-Z-Boy-style recliner!), I was able to afford the trip.

We arrived in Dublin and rode a bus about an hour to the village of Glendalough, in a lush green valley with two lakes. We got off our bus, crossed a small bridge, and suddenly found ourselves transported back fifteen hundred years. We wandered in hushed silence among ancient stone homes and churches, a stone high tower, and a cathedral, awed at the solemn beauty.

Glendalough was a monastic community that had been formed in the sixth century by Saint Kevin, a young man of royal descent who had originally come to the village to seek God in the solitude of a nearby cave. We hiked around one of the lakes to visit his first dwelling place—a hole about four feet wide and seven feet deep in the rock wall of a cliff. Our guide, an Irish rector, told us that in the winter months

Kevin would stand and pray for hours in the icy waters of the lake with his arms stretched toward heaven. According to local legend, Kevin was once praying in the lake when a blackbird landed in the palm of his hand and laid several eggs. Bizarre as all of this may sound, I found my heart strangely moved by Kevin's earnest devotion to God.

After spending a long time in prayer, Kevin sensed God leading him to return to society to spread the good news about Jesus. He began by teaching a single family about the way of God, but this group soon grew to include dozens of families. Seeing the need for a central place from which to teach, Kevin established a monastery at Glendalough.

Over time, other monks joined Kevin, regularly gathering to pray and chant the Psalms at appointed hours and teaching anyone who came to visit them. Local farmers pitched in to build the stone houses and the cathedral we had seen. Pilgrims came from all over Ireland and Europe to learn from the monks and pray with them. As I was listening to our guide share the stories about Saint Kevin and the Glendalough community, I wanted to slip off my shoes—I felt like I was walking on hallowed ground.

During our pilgrimage, we tried to follow the example of these early monks. We took time to pause each morning and evening to pray the daily office (set times for reading liturgical prayers). We read Scripture, spent time in silence, and learned ancient Celtic prayers. We listened to stories and legends about saints from another time, including Saint Patrick and Bridget of Kildare.

Contrary to the popular assumptions about monks and nuns, Celtic monastics did not *withdraw* from society to spend time alone, isolated from the world. Instead, they built their monasteries close to settlements, on well-known hilltops, or on islands near established sea-lanes so they could practically demonstrate the hospitality of Christ.[1] The Celtic monasteries were not just places of prayer and worship; they also served as hotels, emergency shelters, hospitals, libraries, universities, centers for the arts, and mission-sending bases. These spiritual pilgrims were not just concerned with their own spiritual growth; they were a force for justice and community transformation.[2]

I came away from my time in Ireland with a new respect for monks and their monasteries. Like many, I had assumed that those who made prayer the primary occupation of their life did little practical good for society. I left Ireland with a new sense that it was possible to be both deeply prayerful and powerfully engaged in making the world a better place.

Though I didn't recognize it then, my time in Ireland would eventually lead to a second "conversion" for me, a journey of growing to appreciate the beauty of the monastic way of life.

But my conversion to the monastic way didn't mean I adopted *all* of the particular habits of that ancient path. I didn't start wearing a hooded white robe, nor did I start eating in silence. I lived in a city, would soon be married, and with a church ministry and the ever-growing demands of life, I knew I couldn't just leave my life behind—and God was not calling me to do that.

Instead, I began to ask the question that underlies this book: "Is it possible to follow the monastic way, enjoying God in every area of my life, while immersed in the busy routines of modern life?"

Maybe that's a question you have as well.

BUSHIDO

Sometimes people ask me, "Why would an *Asian* person be interested in a monastic path?" After all, the monastic Christian tradition has its roots in places like Ireland, France, and Italy—not Japan. But there are some interesting parallels I have found between my personal history and the call of monastic life.

Several years ago, I asked our church staff to do some research on their family tree. We did this as a way to better know ourselves and our other team members. While exploring my roots, I discovered something surprising—my own ancestors were Japanese Samurai, warriors who sprang to the defense of their community when their people needed protection. Though most people are familiar with the traditional image of a Samurai as a highly disciplined warrior able to wield a sword with breathtaking dexterity and speed, I also learned that the Samurai were farmers, philosophers, poets, and artists. They lived by a code of honor called *bushido*, a set of rules and practices that guided their life and enabled them to grow into people of wisdom, fortitude, loyalty, compassion, and service. They centered on one purpose: serving their Samurai lord and the community. Their lives were often demanding, brutish, and hard. But much like the ancient Christian monastics, they found that living by a particular pattern of life empowered them to become wise, courageous, compassionate people who served their lord and the common good.

I found myself longing for something similar—a pattern of life that would help me live well, grow, and faithfully serve my Lord, Jesus Christ, and the larger community. As I learned more about the Samurai code of *bushido* and the monastic "rule of life," I saw that both of these ancient cultures had developed something simple, yet profound: a life patterned on proven practices that helped them cultivate their character and contribute to the world.

I don't live in a monastery. Nor am I a Samurai swordsman. I'm just an ordinary guy—a businessman turned pastor who struggles with the same challenges we all face. I am a father and a husband. I am a follower of Jesus. And I understand the challenge of integrating all of these callings into a simple way of life, balancing the various demands I face with wisdom and grace.

But I have found a way to live out my commitment to Christ in each of my different relationships and roles through a life-giving rhythm, what the ancient monks referred to as a *rule of life*. A rule of life is simply a rhythm of practices that empowers us to live well and grow more like Jesus by helping us experience God in everything. Though the word *rule* may sound harsh and confining, I have found that living by a rule has paradoxically freed me to pursue the life I have always longed for—a life of deeper, transforming friendship with Jesus and fruitful contribution to the world.

MOVING FORWARD BY LOOKING BACK

I can only guess why you have picked up this book. Maybe you are feeling overwhelmed by your life right now, struggling to grow as a follower of Jesus in the midst of competing priorities and a crazy schedule. Perhaps you are curious to know more about the monastic way of life but aren't sure if it's practical. When you hear the word *monastic* or *monastery*, you likely think of a relic from a bygone era, something quaint and charming but of little practical use today. What can monks who lived centuries ago in a very different time and place teach us about being a pilgrim of Christ in our world today? So much has changed! And yet, despite the significant differences between our cultures, there is much we can learn from their ancient wisdom. In this book, I will explore how a rule of life—a rhythm of ancient practices—helps us experience the transforming presence of Christ in everything and extend his grace to the world.

As remote as the monastic life may seem to us today, the sixth-century world of Saint Benedict and the Celtic monks had many similarities to our own time. People then, as now, were facing economic uncertainty, high taxes, eroding ethics, and sexual excess. As a young man studying in Rome, Benedict (480–547) became disgusted with the corruption he saw all around him. Yearning to live a holy life, he moved into a cave outside of the city. But even in the obscurity of his cave, Benedict became famous as a holy man; people from all over Europe flocked to see him. He later established a monastery in Monte Cassino which to this day continues to inspire people to walk in the way of Christ. To guide the growing number of monks who wanted to follow his example toward a more Christlike way of life, Benedict wrote a rule to guide them. He went on to establish twelve more monasteries, giving birth to a revolutionary movement.[3]

The world has changed dramatically in the fifteen hundred years since Benedict. Yet today more than ever it needs men and women who are hungry for God; who live in the invisible presence of God more than in the visible presence of their social network; who experience life with God as they work, rest, pray, play, cultivate friendships, raise children, care for aging parents, and walk with the poor.

FOR EVERYONE AND IN EVERYTHING

The monastic life is not an exclusive club reserved for an elite few followers of Christ. It is a path that each of us can embrace. In

Dostoevsky's classic novel *The Brothers Karamazov*, Father Zossima says that the monastic way of life is not just for a special sort of person; it is simply what every person *ought* to be. He is suggesting that every one of us has a monk or nun "embryo" inside of us. We all long for something more than the rat race, rushing through life without ever living. We crave depth, an experience of beauty, truth, and meaning. And while most of us won't take permanent vows in a monastic community, we can each learn to enjoy God's presence in our rhythms of work and rest, study and play, community and solitude.

In the words of a popular worship song:

God in our living
There in our breathing
God in our waking
God in our resting
There in our working
God in our thinking
God in our speaking.[4]

A monastic rule of life can help us learn what it means to live so that we are attuned to God in our everything. A life that does more than pray sporadically, but is *itself* a prayer to God.

A life awakened to God so that the world becomes our monastery.

QUESTIONS FOR REFLECTION AND DISCUSSION

1. When did you first awaken to the belief that a life with God mattered?
2. What are some of the surprising contributions of the monastics, and could you see yourself learning from their example and wisdom?
3. Dostoevsky contends that there is a monk or contemplative in each of us. Do you find this true of your experience? If so, how?

— CHAPTER 2 —

CREATING A SPIRITUAL ECOSYSTEM

In the last chapter I introduced you to the ancient pattern that shaped monastic living called a *rule of life*. I know that the word *rule* has negative connotations for most people. We imagine a stern principal from our childhood who was always enforcing the rules. We think of an unyielding police officer who gave us a ticket for not coming to a full stop at an intersection, even when there were no other cars in sight. For a moment, try not to let the word *rule* put you off.

The word *rule* actually comes from the Greek word that means "trellis."[1] A trellis is a support system for a vine or plant that enables it to grow upward and bear fruit. For a grapevine to produce good grapes it must have a trellis to support and guide its growth or it will slump to the ground. When this happens the fruit tends to rot before it ripens. Grapevines in the wild will use just about anything—a tree or even a rock—as a trellis. *It is part of their nature to seek structure.*

Like a trellis, a rule of life supports and guides our growth. It supports our friendship with Christ so that we bear the fruit of his character and are able to offer his nourishing life to others. The *purpose* of the rule, in this sense, is not to be harsh or confining. It is to cultivate fruit. It serves as a pattern for life that enables us to experience the presence of Jesus in each moment of our lives, empowering us to become people who embody his love to others.

THE GIFT OF GROWTH

We see LeBron James soar to the hoop and dunk a basketball. We listen to cellist Yo-Yo Ma play a dazzling rendition of a Bach suite. And we rightly conclude that God has endowed these people with exceptional talent. Sometimes we assume that people who accomplish extraordinary things in sports, music, or some other field have an invisible river of energy that makes their greatness inevitable. We often presume this is also true of people whom we consider spiritually great. We hear an astonishing story about the love of Francis of Assisi or the sacrifice of Mother Teresa and assume that God has simply endowed them with a special anointing. We like to believe God has given them a special charism because it frees us from feeling that we are actually responsible for playing a part in our becoming like Jesus.

There is no such thing as a "magic pill" that can make you a great athlete or an accomplished musician, a master carpenter or a wise parent. We all know people who have an amazing talent or aptitude but have not realized their potential. The path to greatness, whether pursued consciously or unconsciously, is one that requires a rhythm of disciplined practice.

In the same way that no one becomes a great athlete or musician on the basis of a special talent *alone*, no one becomes like Jesus on the basis of a special gift from God *alone*. People grow — they become who they are — not because God zapped them while they walked across a field but because they make a conscious effort to respond to the grace of God and, with the help of the Holy Spirit, cultivate the gift they have received. Those who flourish in their lives with God have a Spirit-initiated rule of life, a *rhythm of practices* that enables them to welcome and respond to Jesus.

The growth of our spiritual lives is *primarily* God's work. On our own, we can no more produce the fruit of Christ's character in our lives than we can squeeze pebbles into diamonds (John 15:5). Yet despite our foibles and failures, God calls us to play a role in our transformation. He invites us to "work out" our "salvation with fear and trembling," precisely *because* "it is God who works in [us] to will and to act in order to fulfill his good purpose" (Philippians 2:12 – 13). Grace, as Dallas Willard observes, is not opposed to effort but to *earning*.[2] We cannot earn our life with God—it's a gift. But we are to make "*every effort* to add to [our] faith goodness ... knowledge ... and love" (2 Peter 1:5–7, emphasis added).[3]

I live in Vancouver, British Columbia near the Pacific Ocean and I've been out on the water when there is no wind. It's a frustrating experience. You wait ... and wait ... and wait some more. A sailor cannot produce wind, but even when there is no wind, there *are* some things you can do. You can trim the sails and position the rudder so that when the wind finally does come, the boat will move. Without these actions you will not be able to sail even when the wind does come. In a similar way, we cannot generate the wind of the Spirit in our lives, but there *are* things we can do to prepare for the wind of God's Spirit.

To take this image further, I imagine that life with God should feel something like sailing along the jagged coastline of British Columbia with its towering, snow-capped mountains. At times, our relationship with God will feel overcast, cold, and even stormy. And like any sailor, we will need to adjust our sails because of the shifting direction of the wind. Yet our passage with God is also designed to be an experience of breathtaking beauty and joy. As the Westminster Catechism reminds us, we are made "to enjoy God and glorify him forever."

THE IMPORTANCE OF DELIBERATE PRACTICE

In response to God's lavish love toward us, we cultivate a rule of life, a rhythm of practices that will help us experience Jesus and embody his wisdom and love in every sphere of our lives.

The apostle Paul uses the image of athletes practicing as a metaphor for our training to become more like Jesus. He writes, "Everyone who competes in the games goes into strict training. They do it to get a crown that will not last; but we do it to get a crown that will last forever."[4] It would be crazy to think you could win a marathon by simply *trying* on the day of the race and not *training* for it.[5] If you haven't been practicing for the race, you won't be able to run a marathon by simply repeating to yourself, "I am powerful. I am a champion. Nothing can stop me." No amount of positive thinking or even trying *really* hard to run on race day will enable you to successfully complete a marathon. You become the kind of person who is able to complete a marathon by deliberately *training* for one.[6]

My friend Elizabeth Archer Klein, who runs marathons, uses her experience as a runner to distinguish between "trying" and "training":

> "Trying" is saying over and over again that tomorrow will be different but staying mostly in the same old patterns. "Training" is setting up a deliberate pattern of behaviors or habits so that we can change. You only get so fit if you run the same route, at the same speed every day, but if you start a five-day-a-week rhythm of tempo runs, sprints, and long slow distance, with rest days and weight training, throwing in a hill day a few times a month, you get stronger. The key is to train *smarter*. If I just keep saying I will "try" harder the next time I race, there will be little impact. But if I train smarter, I will get faster.

Simply running *a lot* or playing music *a lot* will not necessarily enable a runner or musician to improve. *Deliberate practice* is necessary for a runner or a musician to grow. In order for a person to grow in a craft, she or he must create an ecosystem — an environment that fosters growth. Part of this ecosystem, as we have seen, will include *deliberate* practice. Our spiritual lives are no different. In order to thrive in our life with God we need a spiritual ecosystem that includes deliberate practice.

It is possible to engage in a lot of "spiritual" activity but fail to grow. As Martin Luther noted, we can "pray" the Lord's Prayer hundreds or even thousands of times but not really pray — that is, not meaningfully engage with the living God. We might go to church weekly but not truly worship from our heart or attend to the voice of God. We can do a lot of spiritual activity and not deepen our friendship with Jesus. Ironically, attempting too many spiritual practices at once can actually keep our relationship with Jesus on the surface because we are not able to experience him deeply in any of those activities. It's like speed dating. You can't have a significant conversation with any one person even though, or rather *because*, you're doing *a lot* of "dating."

Having a set of deliberate practices also allows us to build on our strengths and shore up areas of weakness. If we are experiencing a failure of self-control, we might deliberately practice fasting.

Fasting can help us develop the spiritual "muscle" of self-control. With the help of the Holy Spirit, this discipline can help us become people whose bodily appetites do not control us. If we find ourselves overcommitted and distracted, engaging in a daily rhythm of ten or twenty minutes of silent prayer that centers us or meditating on a brief single passage in Scripture (*lectio*) may be a helpful practice.

On the other hand, if we have a naturally contemplative bent and find ourselves spending a disproportionately large amount of time in private prayer and solitude, adding another way of praying may not be helpful. In fact, we might consider decreasing the amount of time we spend in *formal* prayer and perhaps enter into practices of justice or service so we can grow as a contemplative *in action*.[7]

As these examples illustrate, depending on our particular growth needs and season of life, we will use different spiritual practices. There is no simple, mechanical formula to produce spiritual growth: if you do *x*, then *y* will happen. This is why the practices that become part of our rule of life must be Spirit-led and deliberate. As our life circumstances change and the Spirit moves, our disciplines will also change over time.

NOT ONE MORE THING TO DO

I've sometimes heard people say, "I'm so busy; I really can't live that way." Or "I just don't have the discipline to do it." In response, it's helpful to remember that if these practices make our lives feel heavier or become just one more thing to do, in all likelihood we have established a *self*-constructed rule rather than a Spirit-created one. Jesus, after all, tells us that his yoke is easy and his burden is light. He teaches us that under his "yoke"—that is, by following him—we will find rest for our souls (Matthew 11:28–30). Thomas Merton in *New Seeds of Contemplation* wrote that "unnatural, frantic, anxious work, work done under pressure of greed or fear" is "never willed directly by God."[8] Similarly, Evelyn Underhill observes, "Fuss and feverishness, anxiety, intensity, intolerance, instability, pessimism, and wobble, and every kind of hurry and worry—these are signs of the self-made, self-acting soul."[9]

A rule shouldn't make our lives feel busier, even if it leads to new practices. Buddhists who have reflected on the rule of Saint Benedict have observed that the monastic life is structured to implement renunciation.[10] When someone makes a monastic vow, for instance, following the practice of the early church described in the book of Acts, they renounce their right to claim personal ownership of anything. They cede all their possessions to the monastery or give them away to friends or family. While most of us will not be turning over our belongings to a monastery, we may find that living by a rule enables us to dispose of certain things (material ones as well as habits and activities), making our lives feel less cluttered and lighter.

As we begin to create our rule, particularly if our relationship with Jesus is newer, we might add certain spiritual disciplines, but as being with Jesus becomes a more habitual part of our lives, we will likely drop certain disciplines.

Creating a rule in response to the movement of the Spirit may also involve simplifying certain practices so that our *relationship* with Jesus is served.

Gail is a nurse and a mother of two teenagers in our faith community who has recently begun experimenting with a rule of life. She says:

> Over the past three months, I have asked God to help me create a rule. I sense God inviting me to do away with my overly ambitious plans and [he] is showing me that what is most important is having a *relationship* with him, as opposed to getting through a spiritual task. It was hard for me at first to realize that quiet time in conversation with God was more fruitful than hurriedly attempting to get through a certain amount of Scripture.... God has taught me that it is all about the relationship, not about what I manage to squeeze into a day. I think for now, God just wants me to enjoy and appreciate him, and to just explore that side of our relationship.

As Gail's story implies, the spiritual practices are not ends in and of themselves. We don't read the Bible, pray, or perform some "spiritual task" so we can check them off our to-do lists. The practices, rather, create space for us to enjoy company with Jesus. They enable us to receive the life of God and are thus aptly called "a means of grace."

THE GIFT OF A CENTERED LIFE

While the lives of actual, real-life monks are surprisingly quite full and not as idyllic as we might imagine, their daily lives are organized around a rule that helps them keep Christ at the center.

Ideally, each part of a monk's life is given the time it deserves—no less, no more. In a monastery, life is regulated by a bell. Monks are frequently reminded that *their time is not their own*. When the bell rings, they must stop what they are doing and move on to what is being asked of them. Saint Benedict taught that the monk must put down his pen without crossing his *t* or dotting his *i*.[11] This pattern of living teaches monks to recognize that there is a proper time and place to do things—sleep, eat, pray, read, work, play. They learn that each part of their lives helps to form Christ in them. This is just one example of the beauty of living by a rule (or rhythm) of life. We may not have an actual bell to remind us of these things, but we create a pattern of life with daily or weekly reminders that help us recall that our time is not our own and enable us to give each moment the time it deserves. With the constant time pressures of our lives, a rule like this rings through the distraction and calls us to pause and experience Christ.

A foundational part of my own rule is keeping a twenty-four-hour Sabbath once a week. When my Sabbath "bell" rings, I unplug, stop working, and don't do anything related to my work. The rule of keeping a Sabbath frees me to spend time with family and not feel guilty that I am not working. On the flipside, I am committed to working when it is time to work without feeling guilty that I am not with my family. In a very practical way, this rule sets life-giving limits for me. A "monastic bell" enables us to establish our limits without feeling shame.

A CENTERED (THOUGH NOT NECESSARILY BALANCED) LIFE

The goal of having a rule is not to achieve a "balanced life" per se, but to live with Christ at the center of all we do.

Some people pursue balance by trying to make each aspect of life the ideal, preferred size, but this misses the point of the

Christ-centered life. Jesus didn't always live what we might consider a balanced life. He regularly withdrew from the crowds to experience solitude, but after a long day's work he might also take time to welcome and heal the sick.[12] There wasn't a simple, easy-to-follow pattern in his life that he used in every circumstance. So while balance isn't always possible, when Christ is our deep center, our priorities become clearer and we can live with a greater prayerfulness and peace.

Ultimately, a rule can enable us to live our lives, as Thomas Kelly writes, "from a center, a divine Center ... a life of amazing power, peace and serenity, of integration and confidence and simplified multiplicity."[13] A friend of mine once said something that continues to ring in my ears: "The only tragedy in life is not to become a saint." It is not a tragedy to have never lived in a large, beautiful house or to have never hobnobbed with the rich and powerful or to have never traveled to an exotic paradise. The only tragedy in life is not to become a saint, because every follower of Christ has this potential. As we orient each sphere of life toward Christ we can become the saints God calls us to be. We become people who embody Christ's light and love to others. Becoming like Jesus is the *greatest* gift we can offer others.

QUESTIONS FOR REFLECTION AND DISCUSSION

1. What connotations, positive or negative, does the word *rule* have for you?
2. How can a rule of life serve as a trellis to help you flourish in your life with God?
3. What role has deliberate spiritual practice played in growing your faith?
4. In what sense are spiritual practices "a means of grace"?
5. How can a rule of life make us feel lighter? Have you ever personally experienced this?

— CHAPTER 3 —

A RULE THAT BENDS

Every thoughtful person has a pattern of practices or habits, a rhythm he or she lives by—even if they have never put their "rule" into words.[1] Take a moment to think about the "rule" you live by. Perhaps you walk your dog each morning, go to church on Sundays, or have pizza with your extended family on Thursday evenings. These patterns are part of your rule. They reflect something you consciously or unconsciously value: caring for your dog, worshiping in community, spending time with your family.

Monks choose to live a monastic life because they want to organize their lives around a divine center. You may never join a monastery, yet you likely share in that yearning to center your life on Christ. That's why it's important for us to grasp that these intentional rhythms aren't just useful for monks. A rule of life can be a gift for ordinary people in their everyday lives: working mothers, stay-at-home dads, dentists, plumbers, accountants, realtors, students, artists. In fact, the more immersed we are in the world with all the pressures that pull us away from God, the more helpful a rule of life will actually be. So let's take a closer look: what does it look like to *build* a rule?

MY RULE IN TOKYO

After completing my undergraduate studies, I began working for Sony in Tokyo, Japan. After a simple breakfast of eggs and tofu, I would slip into my suit and leave my apartment at seven in the morning to catch the subway downtown. I would spend the rest of my day teaching English, Western culture, and business protocol to "salary-men" (corporate soldiers), some of whom would later be dispatched to North America or Europe. Most days, I would arrive home after 11:00 p.m., sometimes even later if I had been invited to socialize at a bar. Working six days a week, I was making far more money than I had ever made before, and I regularly compared my income to the graduates of prestigious business schools in the United States. I felt respected and even admired by my colleagues. As a person of Japanese descent, people in Tokyo seemed to have a comfortable familiarity with me. I also exuded a novel appeal since I had spent my formative years in England and North America. Women were drawn to me in a way I had not experienced before. My life seemed charmed.

But I was unhappy, felt restless, and sensed that my soul was withering.

I had never heard of a monastic "rule of life" before, but I began cobbling together something similar out of sheer desperation. First, I made a decision not to work on weekends. Instead I got involved in a small, local church about a ten-minute walk from my apartment. During my morning commute, though yawning and half asleep, I would spend some time praying and offering my workday to God. After about six months in Tokyo, I began running occasionally on weekends and played pickup basketball from time to time at a local university. I began giving a significant amount of my income to the work of God in Japan. Periodically, I took long walks with a Christian friend, and we talked about how our relationship with God was going and how we were dealing with sexual temptations.

My rule, flimsy as it was, helped preserve the most important part of my life, the part that touched everything else: life with God. Although I wasn't conscious of it at the time, in my desire to live by a rule I was walking in an ancient tradition, one that precedes even the early church fathers and mothers, one that goes back at least as far as ancient Babylon.

DANIEL'S RULE OF LIFE

Daniel is the first person in the Bible we know of who consciously lived by a rule of life. The book of Daniel opens in the year 586

BC, the year Daniel's homeland of Judah is besieged by King Nebu-
chadnezzar of Babylon. Following their defeat to the Babylonian
army, Daniel and many of his gifted contemporaries are deported
to Babylon. As a young person, Daniel is cut off from his family
and friends, his teachers and mentors, his culture and language. As
a potential leader in the Babylonian Empire, he is sent to the "Harvard" of this new land, where he is immersed in a completely pagan
view of history, science, philosophy, and religion. He is also tutored
in astrology, sorcery, and magic—subjects considered idolatrous in
his homeland of Israel. Potent forces are literally conspiring to pull
Daniel from God. At one point in Daniel's life, the king of Babylon
issues a decree making it a capital offense to pray to any god except
himself. Even when it is a crime punishable by death at the mouths
of ravenous lions, Daniel persists in praying to the living God.

Throughout his life Daniel carries out his work for the government with unparalleled wisdom, enabling him to make a profound
contribution, eliciting both the admiration and envy of those around
him. People who don't even believe in his God point to him and say,
"There is a man in whom the spirit of the gods live."[2]

Rather than being carried out to sea by the cultural wave of
Babylon, Daniel is able to remain faithful to God. But how? How
does Daniel become a person whose relationship with God not only
survives but even thrives in such hostile circumstances? It's because
he has a plan to sustain and grow his life with God. He lives by a
rule that guides and shapes his decisions, actions, and response to
circumstances. Daniel makes it his regular practice to return to his
apartment and kneel in prayer three times a day (Daniel 6:10)—
even when he knows this might cost him his life. Daniel centers his
life on God and receives the animating presence of the Spirit, who
energizes him to live faithfully for God in the world.

STARTING TO BUILD YOUR OWN RULE

You may be thinking, "Okay, this spiritual rule thing worked for you
and Daniel. But where do I begin?" To help us visualize the process,

let's return to the trellis imagery I introduced in chapter two and attach the "stuff" of our lives to this structure (see Figure 1).

At the rule's (trellis's) base are three "root" practices:

ROOTS:

- **Sabbath**: finding oasis and rest for body and soul
- **Prayer**: deepening your friendship with God
- **Sacred Reading**: feeding on God's Word

Building from that foundation are the day-to-day pieces of life—family and friends, work and play, et cetera. While a rule of life will be *unique* to each person, these components (which I have divided into three categories) are *common* to all:

RELATE:

- **Spiritual Friendship**: companions for the journey
- **Sexuality**: using your sexual energy in healthy ways that honor God's design
- **Family Life**: together for the sake of the world

RESTORE:

- **Care for the Body**: offering your whole self to God and to others
- **Play**: becoming like a child
- **Money**: experiencing money as a servant, not a master

REACH OUT:

- **Work**: finding God on Monday
- **Justice**: bringing heaven to earth
- **Witness**: how a rule leads you up and out

I'll unpack these topics one by one in the rest of the book, but for the rest of this chapter, let's consider eight important guidelines that will help you avoid some of the most common pitfalls when developing a rule of life and thus enable you to flourish on your journey.

Reach out

WORK JUSTICE WITNESS

Restore

BODY PLAY MONEY

Relate

FRIENDSHIP FAMILY
SEXUALITY

SABBATH PRAYER SACRED READING

Roots

Figure 1

1. START SIMPLY

One of the most common mistakes people make when getting started is doing too much too quickly. Change doesn't happen overnight! Begin by adding a small practice that will help you become more aware of God. Set a chime on your watch as a reminder to direct your attention (even for a moment) to God. Begin your day with a brief time of silence to acknowledge your dependence on God. Or take a few minutes in the evening to recollect your day and savor something for which you are grateful. These simple practices can make you more mindful of God.

Small habits can make a big difference. Kathleen Norris cites a study that observed the daily habits of couples in order to determine what produced good, stable marriages. One activity made a consistent difference: embracing one's spouse at the beginning and the end of each day. Apparently, it didn't seem to matter whether or not partners hugged each other passionately or with a wide yawn. The simple ritual of bookending the day with a momentary embrace helped nurture their lifelong bond.[3] Whatever we do repeatedly— even if it's simple—has the power to shape us. The daily habit of spending time with God shapes us. Even if it is brief and not marked with groundbreaking insight or deep emotion—even when it feels perfunctory—it shapes us.

2. BUILD SLOWLY

A sustainable rule of life will be built slowly, tested, and regularly revised.

It won't be helpful to read about a rule and conclude, "I've been a lazy bum. I haven't been very disciplined about prayer, eating, and exercising. Starting tomorrow morning I am going to get up at 4:00 a.m., spend an hour praying and reading the Bible, go to the park, run seven miles, and come back and eat a nutritious breakfast. Then I'll go to work, come home by 6:00 p.m., eat dinner with the family, help Susie with her homework, do my emails, relax by watching part of the football game on TV, and start reading *War and Peace*."

What will happen? First of all, you're probably going to arrive late at work—still hot, sweaty, and stinky because you didn't have time to take a shower. Then you're going to be up until two in the morning trying to complete your rule. And when the alarm goes off at 4:00 a.m., you're going to hit the snooze button repeatedly.[4]

So it's important to build a rule of life slowly, deliberately, and prayerfully.

Look back at the core practices of the rule. Is there one (Sabbath, prayer, spiritual friendship, witness, etc.) that would be most fruitful for you to begin with? Do you sense the Holy Spirit leading you to focus on a particular aspect of the rule?

3. PRUNE REGULARLY

A rule of life isn't primarily about *adding* more things to your life. In fact, a monastic life is structured to implement renunciation. Jesus said, "I am the true vine, and my Father is the gardener. He cuts off every branch in me that bears no fruit, while every branch that does bear fruit he *prunes* so that it will be even more fruitful" (John 15:1–2, emphasis added). If a grapevine isn't pruned it will grow out of hand. The grapes will remain small and the quality of the fruit will diminish.

Pruning "strips us of what is non-essential to the power of God's life rising within us. But it also gathers and focuses energies previously dispersed in draining distractions or even apparently worthy commitments."[5] This pruning experience can be difficult and at times painful. When we say no to something, we will naturally feel a sense of loss and sadness. However, if the pruning is in line with God's good intention for us, even in the midst of grief, we will experience a deeper sense of peace and well-being.

My natural tendency is to add, add, and then add some more! At times my life has been so full that I have not been present to the people or experiences in it. I have found that "more" can be "less." A wise mentor once told me, "If you are going to add something to your plate, consider taking something off it." I once stepped down from serving on the board of a school I love in order to create space for a new role, serving as a trustee for World Vision. What needs to be pruned in your life in order for you to build a sustainable, life-giving rule?

4. BE ENERGY CONSCIOUS

Your rule is unique to you. Some people are more alert in the morning; others can focus better in the evening. As you create your rule, your rhythm of practices, think about the flow of your energy throughout the day.[6] When during the day is your energy most available? When are you most attentive or creative? When do you enjoy being with people most? When is your energy least available? It is, after all, possible to set aside time to pray, to create something, or to be with our spouse or family or friends, but not have the energy to be present.

I find that the best time for me to pray, exercise, and engage in creative work is in the quiet of the early morning. After lunch feels like the right time for me to deal with minor administrative matters and respond to simple emails. Evenings are a good time for me to spend with family and friends as my inner monastic bell has signaled that the workday is over and I can let go of the day's tasks. Your energy levels may be different than mine. If you can, schedule your work, your family time, and your rhythms for prayer and solitude at optimal times for you.

5. CONSIDER YOUR LIFE STAGE

Your rule must also take into account your season of life. When I was a single person, my rule looked different. When I got married, it changed. When I became a parent, my rule took a different shape yet again. A rule for a single person and for a parent of young children ought to look drastically different.

Similarly, seasons of the year may also shape your rule. Some require more sleep during the darker months of winter and cut back some of their activities during this season. The rule of Benedict, for example, allows the monks to get more sleep during the winter months when there is less sunlight. Others feel a burst of energy in September as they associate that time with the beginning of a new school year.

Some may want to begin something new in January or in spring when the days get longer and flowers and trees begin to blossom.

6. STAY FLEXIBLE

Saint Benedict's rule was designed with "a little strictness in order to amend faults and to safeguard love." His rule is also famous for its gentleness and flexibility. He insisted that "in drawing up its regulations, we hope to set down nothing harsh, nothing burdensome."[7]

On my pilgrimage in Ireland, I was impressed to learn that if a monk was fasting and then received an unexpected visitor, he was to break his fast so he could enjoy food with his guest.

Circumstances inevitably change. An important meeting comes up. We get the flu. We might receive some unexpected out-of-town visitors who ask if they can use our sofa bed for the week. If something comes up and we cannot keep our rule for a period of time, there's no need to fret or be anxious. We need a rule that bends. *We don't exist for the rule. The rule exists for us.*

We may also find that a practice once helpful in the past no longer seems fruitful. We might consider dropping the practice or trying something more challenging. For example, if you've read through the entire Bible each year for five straight years, this way of reading Scripture may no longer feel fresh to you. You might consider practicing *lectio* as a way to prayerfully meditate on a brief passage (described in chapter six) or memorizing a part of Scripture so you can internalize it.

7. MAKE TIME FOR FUN

A rule of life will also include times of fun that bring joy. My wife Sakiko encourages me to do things I really love to do. Like some of my ancestors, I can tend to think, "Life is work and work is life." My existence can easily become all work and no play. Reflecting the holistic wisdom of her native Japan, my wife reminds me that when you do what you love, your body experiences healing. She encourages me to run in the woods with our beloved golden retriever, to sail, and to do other things that bring me life. Ideally, our rule will include things that bring renewal and refreshment.

8. INCLUDE COMMUNITY

A rule of life is meant to be lived out in community. Though Benedict began his spiritual quest in a cave, he didn't stay there. He formed a community and never suggested that life as a hermit living in a cave was the best way to grow closer to God. He knew that a person was most likely to be formed in a "school of love" — a community where people learn firsthand to offer and receive care. Without some kind of community or relationship, we will have no inspiration and support to experience sustained change.

In fact, says author Alan Deutschmann in his book *Change or Die*, it is impossible for us to experience lasting change unless we are in some kind of relationship. Deutschmann notes the research of Dr. Edward Miller, dean of the medical school at Johns Hopkins University, who found that two years after surgery, 90 percent of coronary-artery bypass patients had *not* changed their eating or exercise habits even when their lives were at stake. Yet, whereas only one out of ten people in the overall study changed their habits, eight out of ten people who were surrounded by a *supportive community* were able to make necessary lifestyle adjustments.[8]

A similar dynamic occurs in our spiritual lives. If we want to experience ongoing transformation in Christ, it will most likely happen in the spiritual ecosystem of a loving, supportive community. It is ideal if you have a "coach" — a spiritual director, small group leader, or friend who is a little farther down the road — who can guide and encourage you in your practices. The writer of the book of Hebrews also knew the power of community to help us overcome a different sort of heart disease: "See to it, brothers and sisters, that none of you has a sinful, unbelieving heart that turns away from the living God. But encourage one another daily, as long as it is called 'Today,' so that none of you may be hardened by sin's deceitfulness."[9] Is there someone or a small group of people you could invite to pursue this rule-of-life journey with you?

As noted earlier, in the following chapters I will trace out the practices which comprise a typical rule of life—Sabbath, prayer, sacred reading, friendships, sexuality, family life, care for the body, play, money, work, justice, and witness—and give you an opportunity to begin crafting your own. Because a rule of life is ideally developed in one area at a time, these chapters can be read in any order. And don't forget that developing your rule is not a gimmick, a technique, or a shortcut to spiritual growth. It's a rhythm of spiritual practices that helps center your life on Christ, enabling you to become more receptive to the work of the Spirit. As William Wilberforce, the British MP who tirelessly fought to dismantle the slave trade in the nineteenth century, once said, "There is no shortcut to holiness. It must be the business of our entire lives. So let us begin."

QUESTIONS FOR REFLECTION AND DISCUSSION

1. If every person lives by a conscious or unconscious rule, how would you describe your current rule?
2. What impresses you about Daniel's rule of life? Is there someone whose rule you admire?
3. What is the value of actually crafting a rule of life?
4. Considering the trellis illustration, is there a part of the rule that would be especially fruitful for you to focus on now?
5. As you build your rule, which of the eight guidelines will be especially pertinent for you to remember?
6. Do you sense it would be helpful for you to live out your rule with another person or in a small group? If you resist that idea, why do you think that is so?

PART 2
ROOTS

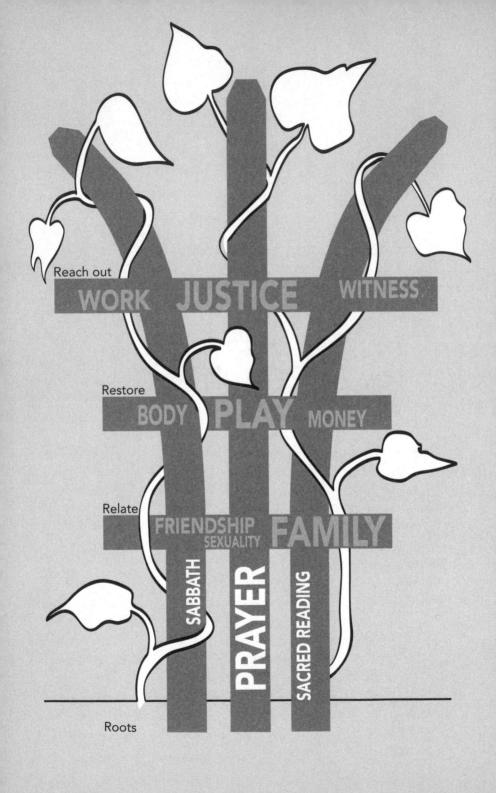

— CHAPTER 4 —

SABBATH: OASIS FOR BODY AND SOUL

One Monday morning several years ago while I was working in Tokyo, I asked a young Japanese salary-man named Hiroshi, "What did you do last weekend?" Hiroshi responded, "Well, I worked really late on Friday and I didn't know what time it was when I woke up, and when I realized it was sometime in the afternoon, I decided to go back to sleep, and slept almost all day Sunday."

Hiroshi's response might sound a little unusual, but most of us wouldn't think much of it. But Hiroshi's colleagues found his story so riveting that they were at a loss for words. They unanimously reverted to the pre-linguistic guttural moans of approval that are unique to the Japanese language: "eeeehhh" (moving from a low to high tone), while nodding vigorously. Hiroshi's Japanese colleagues admired and even envied the way he had spent his weekend. Why? Because Japanese workers are so sleep deprived that they fantasize about sleep in the same way hostages fantasize about food.

You may not be as sleep deprived, but you've likely said to yourself at one time or another, "I am too busy" or "I wish I had more time." You may have fantasized about escaping to a faraway tropical island where you could be free from all your current responsibilities or have daydreamed of taking an early retirement. You may be mentally consumed with a relationship issue, a financial matter, a health concern, a nagging sense of self-doubt, or are troubled by a vague anxiety that you are not doing enough. We long for rest: rest not only for our bodies but for our minds and souls as well. Woven into the very fabric of our beings is a need for regular rest and recovery. God calls us to honor his design for us by living in sync with the gift of Sabbath rest.

Monastic communities have long recognized our innate need for a rhythm of work and rest. Saint Benedict's rule contains two chapters devoted to the Sabbath day,[1] and monasteries today continue to observe Sunday as a special day of celebration. Monks do not engage in manual labor on the Sabbath. Instead, they enter into a time of rest and recreation.

Sabbath keeping is an essential starting point for our rule of life, a necessary "root" to support the rest of our trellis. And so I have intentionally placed this chapter first. When we regularly pause from our ambitions and activities, we create space to experience Christ.

THE GIFT OF ONE DAY IN SEVEN

Thomas Merton says the most pervasive form of violence in the modern world is busyness ... not drugs, not guns, but busyness.[2] The Chinese character for *busy* 忙 combines the pictographs for *heart* and *death*, suggesting that busyness kills the heart. Time flows in seven-day cycles. God's design, as we see in the creation story, is that we work for six days and rest for one. When we violate this rhythm of rest, we damage ourselves and deprive those we love.

Ironically, many of us feel that we are too busy to take time for a Sabbath day once a week. Perhaps you agree that Sabbath is a good thing, even important, but actually practicing it on a weekly basis is more difficult. When was the last time you stopped work and really unplugged from all your electronic gadgets for a day—or even part of a day?

Sabbath reminds us that God invites us to stop. In fact, it's more than an invitation—it's a command. Wayne Muller wisely says, "We stop because it is time to stop. Sabbath requires surrender. If we only stop when we are finished [our emails, our projects], we will never stop—because our work is never completely done."[3] Eugene Peterson observes that nothing less than the force of a commandment has the power to make us stop.[4] In Exodus 20:9–11, God says: "Six days you shall labor and do all your work, but the seventh day is a sabbath to the LORD, your God. On it, you shall not do any work.... For in six days, the LORD made the heavens and the earth, the sea, and all that is in them, but he rested on the seventh day. Therefore, the LORD blessed the Sabbath day and made it holy." Here we see that the Sabbath is patterned on the first days of creation, on a rhythm that predates both Christianity and Judaism. Sabbath keeping is not merely good advice for you to lead a nicely-balanced life. It is a practice that is knit into the created order.[5]

SABBATH AS RESPONSE TO OUR CULTURE OF BUSYNESS

Sabbath, as the foundation of a rule of life, gives you permission to stop from your busyness and simply be. To paraphrase Mark Twain, "Our busyness is like the weather. Everyone complains about it, but no one does anything about it." Instead of complaining about our busyness or assuming it's just a fact of life, we need to ask ourselves *why* we are so busy. Sabbath helps us to question our assumptions.

The truth is that we may be busy because we feel a need to validate our worth. Sabbath gives us a chance to step off the hamster wheel and listen to the voice that tells us we are beloved by God. The Sabbath heals us from our compulsion to measure ourselves by what we accomplish, who we know, and the influence we have. Sabbath enables us to define ourselves less by our achievements and more as beloved daughters and sons of God. As we become more aware of how much we are cherished as children of God, we grow in our trust of God.

SABBATH IN OUR RULE OF LIFE

Sabbath offers us a "sanctuary in time."[6] In keeping Sabbath, we express our love for God by trusting that he will provide for us even while we are resting. Eugene Peterson points out that the Hebrew concept of a day actually begins with evening, not with morning as we are accustomed to thinking. This means that each day begins with the rhythm of evening sleep and rest before the daylight hours of work and activity.[7] After we sleep, we awaken to find that God has been working while we have rested: making dew-covered spiderwebs, cherry blossoms, and puppies.

We learn that even though God doesn't sleep, we can. Understanding that God provides for us in our sleep, we are freed to live with less anxiety.[8] We work from a place of rest, rather than desperately needing rest from our work. We are human beings, not human doings.

SABBATH FOR A STUDENT

Marva Dawn, author of *Keeping the Sabbath Wholly*, learned how to trust God as a student in a demanding PhD program at Notre Dame. Her graduate degree required her to take French, German, and Latin—all at the same time! She recalls:

> After only six weeks of class, I had to be able to translate a thousand words in a two-hour test in each language.... Toward the end of the week, the knowledge that Sabbath would soon come gave me incredibly powerful comfort and courage to persist, even as, at the beginning of the week, memories of the Sabbath delight I had just experienced motivated me to begin again. And on Sundays ceasing to work at languages set me free for lots of fun.... Every Sunday I enjoyed worship and Bible study, ate different foods than I ate during the rest of the week and engaged in relaxing and creative activities. Sometimes I played the organ for worship, went to the beach or swimming pool, took long walks, or played in the parks in the afternoon with friends or by myself. Most of all, Sunday was a day for enjoying God's presence.

Even though her life is "not as intense" right now, Marva says that each week she still experiences a lovely moment of release when she goes to bed on Saturday nights. She observes, "I sleep differently on Saturday nights because the Sabbath has begun."[9]

When I was in graduate school—and before having ever read Marva's book—I too felt convicted to honor the Sabbath commandment by taking a twenty-four-hour period away from study once a week. Because I had exams from time to time on Monday morning, I decided I would take Sabbath from dinner time on Saturday to Sunday evening dinner. Sabbath enabled me to study more effectively the other six days and made school feel less like a grind and more like a gift.

SABBATH IN THE WORKPLACE

My friend Ben began to work at Microsoft when it was still a small company. He loved the exhilaration of working there, but he and his wife Mei-Ling were just beginning a family (they now have four children). As a couple, they agreed he would consistently limit his work to forty hours per week instead of the eighty that employees were expected to put in. When Ben told his boss, his boss paused and said, "Okay, but this will limit your career path." Ben felt conflicted. There was a part of him that didn't want to be absorbed into his work, but there was also a strong desire to fit in, to work the long hours to become a Microsoft "insider." Throughout his time at Microsoft, Ben and his wife prayed that God would grant him favor and make him more productive in the hours he was working. And God answered this prayer. Ben ended up advancing in the company and became a key leader in the development of Windows 95, 98, and 2000. Unlike many of his colleagues, he did not burn out.

There are no guarantees that if we keep the Sabbath we will be successful. But honoring the Sabbath (and not overworking the other six days) will give us an opportunity to grow in our trust of God and experience his faithfulness. If we take time to honor the Sabbath we may actually find that we are less productive than we were before. Like Ben's supervisor warned, our choice to take Sabbath may limit our career path. God's provision for us as we honor his rhythms may be the grace to accept being passed over for a promotion, while gaining a greater sense of fulfillment as we do our work more aware of God, ourselves, and the people around us.

WHAT CAN WE ENJOY ON THE SABBATH?

One of the most practical questions we can ask is, "What is and what is not permissible on the Sabbath?" According to the Hebrew Scriptures, all work was forbidden on the Sabbath. Honoring God and our design for Sabbath means that we cease from work—and activities that closely resemble our work.

Several years ago, Dr. Haddon Robinson, one of my former seminary professors, came to speak at our church in Vancouver. Dr. Robinson grew up in Harlem, New York, and he doesn't hesitate to tell you exactly what's on his mind. While we were having lunch, he said to me, "I am going to give you some unsolicited advice. Take a day off. At least once a week, take a day off. Are you doing that?" At the time, I wasn't.

I stammered, "Well, er, yeah, I think so. I usually take Mondays off, but on Mondays I may do other work, like work on some article that is not related to Tenth."

"Sabbath means that you do something on that day that is *different* from what you have to do the rest of the week," Robinson said. "Working on an article is too similar to the kind of work you do on the other six days. You have to take a day where you do things that are *different* from what you have to do the other six days."

I took his wise words to heart.

Honoring the Sabbath by refraining from work also implies that we should avoid commerce. Without being legalistic, I would suggest we do away with grocery shopping on our Sabbath and minimize our buying in general on that day so that we can savor the gifts we cannot buy—the priceless gifts of God, his Son Jesus, our friends, family, and creation. I realize that some people grew up in strict homes where the Sabbath was a dreary day filled with lots of "don'ts": don't play baseball, don't play games, don't chew gum. In Jesus' day, the teachers of the law multiplied the rules and regulations around the Sabbath so that it was no longer a joy, but a burden; no longer a delight, but a duty. Jesus responded to this dreary view by saying, "The Sabbath was made for people, not people for the Sabbath."[10]

Jesus chose life on the Sabbath: he healed people; he fed them; he supported rescuing animals that fell into wells on the Sabbath. Mark

Buchanan, in his book *The Rest of God*, says that the golden rule for the Sabbath is to cease from what is necessary and to embrace what gives life:

> Sabbath … is a reprieve from doing what you ought to do, even though the list of oughts is infinitely long and never done. Oughts are tyrants, noisy and surly, chronically dissatisfied. Sabbath is the day you trade places with them: they go into the salt mine and you go out dancing.… You get to willfully ignore the many niggling things your existence genuinely depends on—and is often hobbled beneath—so that you can turn to whatever you've put off and pushed away for lack of time, lack of room, lack of breath. You get to shuck the "have-tos" and lay hold of the "get-tos."[11]

Obviously there are times when we *will* have to do what is necessary on the Sabbath—we may have to take our kid to the doctor or shovel snow from the sidewalk in front of our home so that our neighbors aren't imperiled—but as a general rule, Mark's insight is correct. On Sabbath, choose to ignore the "oughts" and attend to what brings life.

WHAT DOES CHOOSING LIFE ON THE SABBATH LOOK LIKE?

Honoring the Sabbath and choosing life means we do something *different* on our Sabbath than what we do the other six days of our week. My brother-in-law Dylan is a professor at the University of California at Riverside. He teaches, researches, and writes—his work involves a lot of mental effort. For him, Sabbath means fishing. This hobby is very restorative for him. If Dylan were a fisherman, fishing probably wouldn't be a restorative Sabbath activity. If you're a student, reading a textbook you have to read may be violation of the Sabbath. Going to the gym to exercise may be a good way to celebrate Sabbath instead. It's important for us to be *honest* with ourselves about our work.

Nancy Woodhull, the founding publisher of *USA TODAY*, was a busy, successful executive. "I am not the kind of person," she once explained, "who can just sit around the pool and not do anything, so I take a dictaphone to the pool, and when I have ideas I record them. People will say to me, 'Nancy, why don't you relax and recharge?' I reply, 'I am being energized by getting these ideas down.' Having access to a dictaphone [smartphone and laptop] allows you to be more productive. There is really no need for down time."

Less than a decade after she described her modus operandi, she died of cancer. She was only fifty-two. There is no way, of course, to determine conclusively whether there was a direct relationship between Woodhull's work habits and her early death, but her profile was not significantly different from many Japanese people who die from *karoshi* (death from overwork).[12]

Ideally, we enjoy our work. Yet we are called to set aside our work and anything related to it for one day in seven. To disregard the Sabbath by working seven days a week not only dishonors God but also God's good intention for us.

RE-CREATION

I love to spend time outdoors. I remember asking a respected author on the spiritual life, Dallas Willard, if he thought it would be appropriate for me to go on long mountain bike rides on the Sabbath as part of my day off. Dallas asked me, "Do you mountain bike because you feel you *need* to do that to stay in good condition?" "No. I run most days to stay in shape." "Are you training for a race?" "No, I just like to mountain bike recreationally. I just love doing it." "Then I think it's fine for you to ride," Dallas concluded.

I also love the water. Swimming, sailing, and kayaking are prayerful experiences for me. Others may savor art, music, or reading on their Sabbath. What is life-giving for you? Choose those leisure activities that make you most alive, drawing you closer to God. Even if the activity itself is done in solitude, it will likely enable you to become more available for others afterward. Our Sabbath rule will set us free to enjoy God and glorify him in all things. It is a day to eat different foods; take a nap; spend time with people you love; make love; enjoy nature, sports, or music; worship and celebrate God and his gift of life with others. Sabbath is about shucking have-tos and allowing God to re-create you.

IS RECREATION ENOUGH?

While leisure and recreation are important, leisure *alone* will not bring us the deepest and most profound kind of rest. Someone recently told me, "I can be lying down at the pool and within fifteen seconds I can be thinking of all the things I *ought* to be doing." When we are relaxing, we can sometimes feel like we ought to be doing something more productive and the voice of self-condemnation reverberates in our souls.

Studies have shown that it is possible to sleep, but if we don't experience REM sleep, the deeper "rapid eye movement" sleep, we won't feel deeply rested. This tells us that it is not just sleep, but the quality of the sleep that counts. In order to deeply rest, we need more than simply the absence of work. We need to experience *internal* rest.

And so it is with our lives. We need not just rest but a certain quality of rest: deep inner rest, rest from the inner murmur that says we are defined by what we do, what we have, or by what others think of us. Part of the reason we can't truly find rest is that we are trying to validate our existence to ourselves or to other people. To experience full rest, we need to be free from the voice of self-condemnation.

One of my all-time favorite films is *Chariots of Fire*, based on the true story of Eric Liddell. Liddell was a devoted follower of Christ who represented Great Britain at the 1924 Olympic Games in Paris. Liddell lived at a time when people believed that the Sabbath was to be observed on *Sunday*. As a committed Christian, Eric Liddell honored his conscience and withdrew from the 100-meter race, his best event—the one for which he was the odds-on favorite to win the gold medal—because the qualifying heats were on a Sunday. Liddell was naturally disappointed that he was not able to compete in the 100 meters because he wanted to honor his homeland, Scotland, with a gold medal and because he simply loved to run. Yet he had peace with his decision because his life was not *defined* by winning a gold medal at the Olympic Games, but by the fact that he was beloved by God.

In stark contrast to Eric Liddell, Harold Abrahams was competing in those same Olympic Games. Abrahams did not have Eric Liddell's faith, and was an intense, driven man. In the film, as he anticipates running for Olympic gold, he discloses his true motivation for racing to his teammate Aubrey: "I'm forever in pursuit and I don't even know what I am chasing . . . I have ten lonely seconds to justify my existence [by winning the gold medal]."

Most people have an easier time relating to Harold Abrahams than to Eric Liddell. We feel we have to *do* something to justify our existence. At school, at work, or as parents in the home we feel like we need to outrun our peers to validate our worth. Or we feel like we need to have something or to be with somebody to justify our existence. Even when we are "resting," we are not really resting. We're lying out at the pool and thinking of what we ought to be doing. We are not experiencing the REM sleep of the soul.

WORSHIP

We honor Sabbath most fully when we gather with God's people to pray, worship, sing, listen to the stories of Scripture, and immerse ourselves in the reality of our Creator. We truly experience Sabbath when we orient our lives not around ourselves but around Jesus and listen and respond to his invitation: "Come to me, all you who are weary and burdened, and I will give you rest. Take my yoke upon you and learn from me, for I am gentle and humble in heart, and you will find rest for your souls."[13] Worship is an essential part of Sabbath and central to our rule of life. It is by turning to God that we are reminded that the core truth of our identity is not what we do or what we have or what others think of us, but the fact that we are beloved by God. Worship quiets the restless inner voice of self-condemnation and renews our vision of God's love. Once we understand that, we can experience true rest for both our body and our soul.

QUESTIONS FOR REFLECTION
AND DISCUSSION

1. Why is it difficult for many of us to take a weekly Sabbath?
2. How is the Sabbath commandment an expression of God's love for us? How is keeping the Sabbath a subversive, countercultural act?
3. What "necessary" things will you relinquish on your day of rest? How might some planning help you more fully enter into Sabbath rest?
4. What would choosing life look like for you on the Sabbath?
5. How does honoring the Sabbath help us grow in our trust of God?
6. Why is worship essential to experiencing true REM spiritual rest?

NOTE: The last page of all remaining chapters provides space for you to reflect on and begin writing your own rule of life.

WRITING YOUR RULE

As you begin drafting your rule of life, write down what day would best serve as your Sabbath and how you might spend it. Is there also a retreat or vacation rhythm that you could pencil in as part of your rule? (Sample rules of life can be found in the appendix.)

— CHAPTER 5 —

PRAYER: DEEPENING YOUR FRIENDSHIP WITH GOD

When I was in the sixth grade I had a crush on a girl named Kristy. During the summer months, I rode my bike to her house three or four times a week, and we would sit on the grass under the warm sun, jump on her trampoline, eat donuts, and drink Coke. It was a blissful, magical time.

But what did I know about relationships? Next to nothing. *One* thing I did know was that if you want to get to know someone, you need to get on your bike, go to their house, and spend time with that person. Friendships take time. And if we want to grow our friendship with God, we will cultivate a rhythm of spending time with him. We are offered an immeasurable gift. God, the Creator of all things, the One who knows us better than anyone else and yet loves us more than anyone else, invites us to this friendship. Sharing time with God should never be seen as a duty: it's a *get to*, not a *have to*; a *may*, not a *must*.[1]

The rhythm of spending time with God—what we commonly call prayer—is another "root" practice in our trellis that supports every part of our life. Richard Foster says, "Of all the spiritual disciplines prayer is the most central because it ushers us into perpetual communion with the Father."[2] Through prayer we can experience the life and fruit that springs out of our union with Christ. Prayer can transform each activity of life—work, homemaking, study, service, recreation—into something sacred.

After Jesus' original disciples and the apostle Paul, Saint Benedict has been called the most influential Christian for the first one thousand years of church history. The primary purpose of the ancient monastic movement he started, the Opus Dei, was to develop a life of prayer as a work of God and to make work itself a form of prayer. Although the precise phrase is not found in his rule, Benedict's perspective can be summarized in the famous dictum, "To pray is to work; to work is to pray." Most of us don't live in a Benedictine monastery, so what might this rhythm of prayer and work look like for us today?

A TIME FOR PRAYER

Rhythms of prayer will be shaped by the kind of work we do, our life stage, and our temperament. Morning is the ideal time for me to focus my attention and enjoy friendship with God. I prefer going to bed early and rising early. In the morning I typically go downstairs, make a light breakfast, and sit down at our kitchen table. After several minutes of silence, I put on my headphones and begin listening to a Psalm, a passage in the Gospels, or another Scripture while reading along in my Bible. I YouTube a worship song, usually one from our previous Sunday's worship service, then enter into a time of prayer in response to something that has resonated with me from that passage or song. I almost always follow this routine by jogging or swimming; after quiet contemplation, physical activity feels like an extension of my time with God.

Beginning my day this way works well for me in this season of my life. It's a time I feel fresh and alert. My mind is relatively uncluttered. I make a point of not reading the newspaper or checking email or phone messages first thing in the morning. These things will trigger my mind to recall all the things I feel I ought to do. But a morning rhythm, while helpful for me, may not be suitable *for you*. Some people can't focus well first thing in the morning—especially without coffee. Gordon Smith, a perceptive writer on the spiritual life, wisely says, "I came to realize that a better guiding rule (than praying first thing in the morning) is that we should give the *best* time of our day to God; and by best I mean the time when we are most alert and capable of being present to God."[3]

For some people several brief times of prayer throughout the day work better than trying to pray for a longer block of time. John Cassian, the Desert Father, encouraged people to pray briefly and frequently.[4] He fostered this practice so that his monks would become conscious of God while weaving baskets or working in the fields and learn to pray out of their everyday work experience.

When I was an undergraduate student, I enjoyed doing prayer walks or jogs at about 10:00 or 11:00 p.m. Then, in my mid-thirties, I found I was becoming less alert late at night. As my life became more complex as a parent, I found it even harder to engage in a sustained time of listening to the Scripture and prayer at the end of the day.

Despite my waning energy in the evening hours as I've grown older, I have continued to find one practice helpful to maintain. Every evening I try to set aside five or ten minutes to pray what Saint Ignatius called the prayer of *Examen*. After putting our toddler down, I lie on the futon next to his bed, quiet my thoughts, and hit the "play" button on the video of my day. I think about the people with whom I've spent time, the conversations I've had, the places I've been, and the projects and tasks I've experienced. I try to recall my thoughts and feelings as well—even if I don't understand their significance at the time. I also ask myself, "What am I most grateful for today? Where did I feel most alive, fulfilled, or in sync with God?" I savor that gift and thank God for it. Then I ask myself, "What am I least grateful for today? Where did I feel the most stress, anxiety, or frustration, or what do I most regret?" I offer this to God in prayer. I may ask forgiveness for sin I have committed.

THE DAILY OFFICE

People who grew up in an evangelical church are often familiar with the tradition of a "daily quiet time" which typically involves reading the Scripture and praying at the beginning of the day. But other Christians throughout the history of the church have also found it profitable to pray at *various* intervals during the day. The psalmist says, "Evening, morning, and noon I cry out in distress, and he hears my voice."[5] As noted in an earlier chapter, Daniel, a high ranking government official in Babylon, had a habit of praying three times a day—even when he was risking his life to do so. Following the biblical pattern of praying at intervals throughout the day, monks in Benedictine monasteries pray at seven different times each day. They pray what are called the daily "offices"—established services of prayer—every time the bells chime.

Though most of us will not spend our lives in a monastery, we can still learn from this practice and establish habits that remind us to pray briefly at various times throughout the day. You may have a watch that chimes or can use your smartphone alarm to remind you to pray. Some people use what are called "breath prayers," short prayers that express the deep yearning of one's heart in a natural way.[6] Prayer can also fill the idle moments of our day. Rather than fumbling for our smartphone to check our email, we can use these pauses as an opportunity to attune to God's presence.

My interactions with my wife often occur at various points throughout a day: a couple of brief phone calls while I'm away from the house, catching up on the day over dinner or while doing the dishes together. From time to time we set aside a couple of hours to go out for dinner on our own. On these evenings, we are able to relax in each other's presence, perhaps raising a concern or discussing an important issue more deeply, or simply enjoying unhurried time together. Likewise, we may also find it helpful to periodically set aside longer blocks of time with God to talk to him more thoroughly about an issue in an unhurried way, to listen more attentively, or to simply enjoy his company.[7]

A PLACE FOR PRAYER

Though we can pray anywhere, the place we spend time with God may affect our conversation with him. Most of us will not be able to visit a chapel every day, but making a few simple changes in a bedroom, an office, or even a car can transform an ordinary space into one that fosters prayer. Removing clutter, putting up a work of art or a cross, or placing an icon or a candle on a table can help make a space more conducive for prayer. When one of my seminary professors, Sam Hamilton-Poore, served as a pastor in Iowa he decided to remove the clutter from his office and remake the room by adding a rocking chair and placing meaningful art on the walls. He noticed afterward that people seemed more relaxed and lingered longer in that space. We are bodily creatures; art, beauty, and location matter, even if we are not always aware of them.

POSTURE FOR PRAYER

In C. S. Lewis's *The Screwtape Letters*, a young demon-in-training named Wormwood is instructed by his experienced Uncle Screwtape about the importance of keeping human beings ignorant of the role of the body in prayer: "My dear Wormwood ... at the very least, they [humans] can be persuaded that the body position makes no difference to their prayers; for they constantly forget what you must always remember, that they are animals and whatever their bodies do affects their souls."[8] Our body position shapes the posture of our prayers.

Some of the first followers of Jesus maintained the Jewish habit of standing for prayer with their arms extended and their eyes open wide to the heavens above. Conversely, others kneel or lie prostrate to express reverence before God. Some people have found that sitting in a simple flat-seated chair, back erect and both feet firmly on the floor, helps them pay attention to God. For some people, the stillness of the body facilitates stillness of the mind. Others may prefer to walk and talk with God, just as they would do with a close friend. Physical movement can release restless energy and foster a more contemplative frame of mind.

PRAYER IN COMMUNITY

The church of the first century was dedicated to praying together. When we read Acts 2:42 in its original Greek language we see that the members of the original church devoted themselves to "the prayers." When Luke, the author of the book of Acts, uses the definite article to refer to *the* prayers, we know that he doesn't just have private prayer in mind—he is referring to the prayers of the community when God's people come together for worship.

Dietrich Bonhoeffer in his book *Life Together* encourages us to say our prayers with sisters and brothers in Christ and express our "common petitions, common thanks, common intercessions" to God "joyfully and confidently." As we pray together we find we are steadied and upheld by the prayers of fellow believers.[9]

Have you ever been on a mountaintop alone and observed a breathtaking vista, or visited a beach and witnessed a stunning sunset? Perhaps you wished that you could have shared your sense of wonder with someone you were close to (or even a stranger for that matter) or longed to see their reaction. When we experience something beautiful with others, our joy and sense of gratitude deepens. My wife and I recently went to a U2 concert in Vancouver. We could have listened to the songs at home on our own, but there was something about experiencing music together with others that intensified the experience. Part of the reason people go to a live concert or attend a football game is because they experience something more fully in community than they do on their own. The same is true with prayer. When we pray with others, we experience God in a more complete way than we can on our own.

PATTERNS FOR PRAYER

When we meet someone for the first time, we don't always know what to say or how to engage the person. There may also be times when we are not sure how to converse with God. Having some kind of pattern that guides our prayers helps us, especially when we are learning to pray on a regular basis. I have found a few patterns of prayer that are beneficial in different ways.

THE LORD'S PRAYER

I regularly use the Lord's Prayer (Matthew 6:9–13) as a guide for my prayers. While there are many ways we can pray to our Father in heaven—and although God is astonishingly hospitable—at times we may grow anxious and wonder if we are really communicating to God in the "right way." When we pray the Lord's Prayer, we can pray with confidence, knowing that this is a God-inspired prayer that pleases him. The Lord's Prayer can be prayed word for word or used as a model for prayer. (In Matthew's gospel, Jesus says pray *like* this.) The prayer is brief. It can be prayed in less than a minute—even if prayed slowly. But though it is short, it is broad in scope, encompassing all that we need to pray.

PATTERNS OF PRAYER IN THE LORD'S PRAYER

Our Father in heaven,
hallowed be your name.
Your kingdom come,
your will be done,
on earth as it is in heaven.
Give us this day our daily bread.
And forgive us our debts,
as we forgive our debtors.
And lead us not into temptation,
but deliver us from the evil one.
For yours is the kingdom and the power and the glory forever.
Amen.

Abba. The first word Jesus used in this prayer would have been *Abba*, which means "Father." We begin our prayer with an acknowledgment that we are praying to our loving, good, strong Abba Father. If you are a parent, you likely know how your heart has opened in love toward your daughter or son long before she or he was able to perform anything noteworthy (when their greatest accomplishments were eating, pooing, and sleeping). God's love for us as his daughter or son is the same. He loves us in a way that is independent of anything we can do. As we pray, our hearts can sense that we are cherished by a perfect Father—who is also *our* Father.

The next words are *in heaven*. We pray to a Father who loves us but is also powerful. The phrase *in heaven* points us to a King who reigns over all the earth.

Adoration. The prayer continues, *hallowed be your name*. In Jesus' day, a name implied a person's character or his or her deserved reputation. By praying these words, we acknowledge that God's character is to be honored and revered, and we also express our desire that both we and others would lovingly do so.

Acceptance. We then pray, *Your kingdom come, your will be done*. While we of course have desires and preferences, we open ourselves—as far as humanly possible—to God's loving will and ask for his good purposes to be fulfilled in each area of our lives: our school, our work, and our relationships. We offer these areas to God and pray that his justice and peace would spread throughout the whole world.

Ask. *Give us this day our daily bread*. Here we pray that our basic needs for food, clothing, work, and shelter be met. The plural *our* also suggests we are to pray that God would provide food for the hungry billions across our world.

Forgive us our debts, as we forgive our debtors. Receiving forgiveness is as necessary for the health of our souls as food is for the health of our bodies. As we receive forgiveness, we in turn forgive those who have sinned against us.

Lead us not into temptation, but deliver us from the evil one. Having prayed for our sins to be forgiven, we pray that we would not return to them. We pray that when we are tempted we would not be vulnerable to sin, and when we are vulnerable we ask that we would not have the opportunity to sin.

Postscript. *For yours is the kingdom, and the power and the glory forever, Amen*. Though this postscript may not have been in the original manuscript of Matthew's gospel, it is fitting that we conclude our prayer in worship—acknowledging that our Father is also the Lord of heaven and earth. This concluding thought shifts our focus from ourselves back to the One who sustains all life.

The Lord's Prayer can help to guide and offer balance to our prayers.

PRAYING ACTS

I was taught as a new believer to pray using the acrostic ACTS, a pattern that lays out the basic elements of the Lord's Prayer in a helpful, easy-to-remember progression: Adoration, Confession, Thanksgiving, and Supplication. Like the Lord's Prayer, this pattern of prayer begins with adoring and worshiping a God who is truly worthy of our praise. It shifts the focus from ourselves and places it on the ever-present God. It then creates space for us to acknowledge and confess our sins and experience a sense of God's forgiveness anew. The prayer also guides us into a time of thanksgiving as we recall the blessings in our lives and express our gratitude to the Giver of these gifts. From this place of thankfulness, we enter into supplication, presenting requests to God for ourselves, our friends and family, our work and world. The ordering of this prayer is intentional. Many times, after having worshiped, confessed sin, and recalled God's many gifts, the kind of requests I make at the end of the prayer are different, truer to my real situation.

PRAYING THE PSALMS

The Psalms also provide a rich portfolio of patterns for prayer. While the other books of the Bible primarily convey God's word to us, the Psalms model our word back to God. The Psalms have served as the prayer book not only of Jesus but of the Hebrew people and the church since its founding. The 150 individual psalms are enlivening prayers to pray verbatim or to serve as springboards to personal prayer. They express virtually every emotion we experience: joy, gratitude, frustration, anger, envy, lament, guilt, forgiveness, faith, hope. (Even if each psalm does not express our particular desire at the moment, it is expressing the prayer of someone in the body of

Christ.) A mentor of mine describes the Psalms as "the sewage treatment plant for the soul": we can bring any emotion we have to the Psalter and find it somehow purified on the other side. The Psalms give us language to express ourselves honestly to God—something vital to the growth of any relationship. When we communicate to someone only in ways we think are "polite and appropriate," the relationship remains superficial. But when we express our sadness, vulnerability, or anger to someone, our friendship deepens. Praying for the things that are on our hearts is a good beginning point for prayer. Prayer is about sharing our concerns with God—and the concerns of our hearts are also things that concern God.

PATTERNS OF PRAYER IN THE PSALMS

The Psalms help us express a wider range of emotions to God:

- In times when I have felt **conflicted** in my desires, I have prayed Psalm 37:4: "Take delight in the LORD, and he will give you the desires of your heart." I have asked God to give me *his* desires, and from a place of living with his desires I would experience the fulfillment of those desires.
- When I have felt **anger** at God for (seemingly) not responding, I have prayed Psalm 22:2: "My God, I cry out by day, but you do not answer!"
- When I have **sinned**, I have prayed Psalm 51:10: "Create in me a pure heart, O God, and renew a steadfast spirit within me."
- When I have felt **overwhelmed** by some difficulty, I have prayed Psalm 27:1, 5: "The LORD is my light and my salvation—whom shall I fear? The LORD is the stronghold of my life—of whom shall I be afraid?... For in the day of trouble he will keep me safe in his dwelling; he will hide me in the shelter of his sacred tent and set me high upon a rock."
- And when my heart has welled up in **gratitude**, I have prayed Psalm 107:1: "Give thanks to the LORD, for he is good; his love endures forever."

SEASONS OF PRAYER

Romantic relationships start with a flush of intense emotional feeling. Marriages begin with an actual and metaphorical honeymoon period. In this early stage of a romantic relationship words flow easily. When you walk into a restaurant you can spot the new couples—they are touching each other and engaged in animated, nonstop conversation.

Our prayer life and rule of prayer will be shaped by the different stages of our spiritual journey as well. Many people who have just come to know Christ find that their prayer words flow easily. Prayer is a joy for them. But, as with romantic relationships, there is a natural movement beyond this honeymoon phase. When feelings of intense connection with God ebb, we have a new opportunity to engage God—not based on cool spiritual vibes but as an expression of our genuine love for God. Times of spiritual dryness are normal for almost everyone, even if we haven't sinned and to the best of our knowledge haven't done anything to wall off our relationship with God. God may allow this dryness so that we can mature in our relationship with him and learn to seek him not for an ecstatic spiritual experience but out of a deeper love and commitment.

SILENT PRAYER

As our relationship with God deepens, words continue to be important, but they become less essential. "Prayer is like love. Words pour at first," says Carlo Caretto, "then we are more silent and can communicate in monosyllables. In difficulties a gesture is enough, a word, or nothing at all—love is enough. Thus the time comes when words are superfluous.... The soul converses with God with a single loving glance, although this may be accompanied by dryness and suffering."[10]

Our deepest prayers transcend words. The Holy Spirit prays through us in groans that are too deep for words (Romans 8:26–27). During times when we find it difficult or impossible to pray with words, we can remain silent before God, trusting that the Holy Spirit is praying in us and cultivating our friendship with God.

While serving as a pastor in Maryland, Eugene Peterson used to spend his days off hiking along a river or on a mountain with his wife Jan. Before their hike they would read a psalm and pray. They would then hike in complete silence for the next two or three hours, until they broke for lunch. In their silence they would experience communion not only with the river, the oak trees, and granite boulders—and with their Creator—but also with each other. Close couples, twins, and intimate friends can feel comfortable with each other in silence and can say much even when exchanging very few words.

As our relationship with God grows, we too can pray without using many or any words. As our awareness of the Divine Presence grows, we can simply enjoy this friendship. Instead of experiencing prayer as something we do, we can savor God and receive. There may be times when, as Basil Pennington says, *saying* our prayers gets in the way of prayer.[11] There are times when silence is the most appropriate posture before God.

The psalmist affirms this truth: "Be still and know ..." that God is God.[12]

The Indian Jesuit Anthony DeMello tells a parable called "The Little Fish."

> "Excuse me," said an ocean fish. "You are older than I, so can you tell me where to find this thing they call the ocean?" "The ocean," said the older fish. "It is the thing you are in now." "Oh, this? But this is water. What I'm seeking is the ocean," said a disappointed fish as he swam away to search elsewhere.[13]

God is present everywhere. We know that God's Spirit dwells within us, as followers of Jesus. This means that prayer is less about *looking* for God and more about cultivating an ever-growing awareness of his presence. In prayer we discover what we already have. We start from where we are and deepen what we already have, and we realize we are already there.... Everything has been given to us in Christ. All we need is to experience what we already possess.[14]

QUESTIONS FOR REFLECTION AND DISCUSSION

1. In what ways is growing your prayer life like deepening a friendship?
2. Is there a pattern of prayer that resonates with you? What are the gifts and potential pitfalls with using patterns for prayer?
3. Do you agree that praying with others can amplify our awareness of God? Have you ever had this experience?
4. How might silence play a role in your prayer life?

WRITING YOUR RULE

What times work best for you to pray? Based on this, draft a daily or weekly rhythm of prayer.

— CHAPTER 6 —

NOURISHING YOUR SOUL THROUGH SACRED READING

When my wife Sakiko was a young girl living in Osaka, Japan, she loved mandarin oranges. Once while eating mandarin oranges, one after another, after another . . . her mother teased her by saying, "You're turning orange." Whether Sakiko really did become a shade of orange or whether her mother was simply trying to persuade her to exercise some moderation, it's true that we become what we eat. Since our bodies are continually shedding cells and producing new ones from the things we eat, what we eat literally becomes us. This is equally true in the realm of spiritual realities: the spiritual food we digest will determine the person we become. Jesus said that we do not live on bread alone, but on every word that comes from the mouth of God.[1] As we feed on God's Word, it nourishes us and becomes part of us.

The third and final "root" practice of the trellis, the rule of life that shapes our spiritual growth, is regularly reading God's Word. Psalm 1 describes the person who continually feeds on God's Word as one who is truly blessed, a happy person, or as Eugene Peterson says, a person with "holy luck."[2] Take a moment to read this psalm out loud:

[1] Blessed is the one who does not walk in step with the wicked
or stand in the way that sinners take or sit in the company of

mockers, [2] but whose delight is in the law of the LORD, and who meditates on his law day and night. [3] That person is like a tree planted by streams of water, which yields its fruit in season and whose leaf does not wither—whatever they do prospers. [4] Not so the wicked! They are like chaff that the wind blows away. [5] Therefore the wicked will not stand in the judgment, nor sinners in the assembly of the righteous. [6] For the LORD watches over the way of the righteous, but the way of the wicked leads to destruction.

I invite you to read this passage aloud one more time, slowly, pausing and praying in response to any word, phrase, or image that has energy for you or speaks to you.

CHEWING THE WORD

In Psalm 1, the blessed person is one who meditates on God's Word. The Hebrew word for "meditate" is *hagah.* Isaiah uses this word to refer to the sounds that a lion makes over its prey.[3] Eugene Peterson in *Eat This Book* offers a vivid metaphor that helps us better understand the background to this phrase:

> Years ago I owned a dog who had a fondness for large bones. Fortunately for him we lived in the forested hills of Montana. Later he would show up on our stone, lake-side patio carrying or dragging his trophy, usually a shank or a rib; he was a small dog and the bone was often as nearly as large as he was.... He would prance and gambol playfully before us with his prize, wagging his tail, proud of his find.... He gnawed the bone, turned it over and around, licked it, worried it.... He was obviously enjoying himself and in no hurry. After a leisurely couple of hours he would bury it and return the next day to take it up again. An average bone lasted about a week.[4]

As Psalm 1 reminds us, the blessed person is the one who meditates on the Word of God, gnawing and sucking its marrow, growling with delight over it.

The author of Psalm 1 also tells us that the blessed person is like a tree planted by streams of water, which yields fruit in season and whose leaf does not wither (v. 3). A tree planted by a stream is fed by the flowing water and the sun in ways that are not immediately perceptible to the eye: water nourishes the tree's roots, the soil provides the roots with minerals, and the sun nurtures the tree as it activates photosynthesis. As water, soil, and the sun nourish a tree, so the Word of God nourishes our souls.

When I first became a follower of Christ as a teenager, even though I generally hated reading I found that I had an enormous hunger for Scripture. I began to meditate on passages in the Word and even memorized parts of the Sermon on the Mount (Matthew 5–7) and 1 John. As I spent time reading the Bible, my faith in God grew stronger. A. W. Tozer in *The Pursuit of God* says, "The Bible is not an end in itself, but a means to bring men [and women] to an intimate and satisfying knowledge of God, that they may enter into Him, that they may delight in His Presence, may taste and know the inner sweetness of the very God Himself is the core and center of their hearts."[5] Jesus said to the religious elite of his day, "You study the Scriptures diligently because you think that in them you have eternal life. These are the very Scriptures that testify about me, yet you refuse to *come to me* to have life" (John 5:39–40, emphasis added). The ultimate end of Scripture is not the text itself but an intimate, joyful, nourishing friendship with the living God. The written Word helps us encounter and unite with the living God.

MEDITATION

But how do we actually meditate on the Word? What does this look like? Saint Benedict offers us a practical model for meditating on Scripture through another ancient practice called *lectio divina*: a hungry, prayerful reading of the Bible. *Lectio divina* is a way of coming to the Bible, not like a computer manual that we feel obligated to plow through, but as a personal letter that we ponder and savor. When we practice *lectio divina*, our reading naturally leads to meditation, our meditation to prayer, and our prayer to feasting on the living God.[6] In his book *Meditating on the Word*, Dietrich Bonhoeffer says that when you study something you analyze it, but when you receive a word from a loved one, you simply open your heart and savor it as Mary did when she was told by the angel that she would conceive and become the mother of Jesus Christ.[7] When we meditate on the Word, we chew it slowly, letting its meaning spread through our blood.[8]

Meditation takes time. Instead of gliding from one text to another, we focus on just one passage, one phrase, or even a single word. We reflect on it in light of our current circumstances: we allow it to convict and comfort us. We pray it. We revisit it at various points during the day or week or even longer. The goal of meditating on the Word is not to get through as much Scripture as possible but to go deeper so that its truth moves from our heads to our hearts, from study to prayer. As Tozer reminded us, the Bible is not an end in itself but a bridge for us to enter into an intimate and satisfying friendship with God.

My own practice of meditating on the Word is simple. In the morning, over a bowl of cereal, I put on my headphones, turn on my iPhone, and begin to listen to a selection of Scripture. In the summer I walk up Little Mountain, a hill not far from our home, or go to a nearby beach and listen to the Psalms or a passage in the Gospels. If something speaks to me, I'll pause the Scripture on my iPhone, scroll the text back, and replay it a few times. I will reflect on it and pray over it. Recently, I was listening to Psalm 90. It begins with the words: *LORD, you have been our dwelling place throughout all generations.*

As I hear these words I think about my grandmother, my only living grandparent, who is now ninety-seven. She is experiencing memory loss and some of the first signs of dementia, and I am not sure how much longer she will live. I think about how when she dies a whole generation of my family will have passed away. I become conscious of how quickly our lives fly away.

Then I am struck by the words of the psalmist: *Teach us to number our days, that we may gain a heart of wisdom* (v. 12).

I play these words over and over again. They echo through my soul. I grow conscious of how brief our days on earth are, and I start praying for God to give me a heart of wisdom—to not pursue something just because it brings me honor but because it is pleasing to God's heart. Later that morning while swimming laps at the pool, the words *give me a heart of wisdom* come to mind and I offer a brief prayer that God would fill me with his wisdom. As I walk to work, they return to mind yet again. One of the gifts of prayerfully listening to Scripture is that the Word becomes part of who we are; it lodges in the heart and becomes available as food for our journey.

HIDING GOD'S WORD IN OUR HEARTS

In Psalm 119:11 we read: "I have hidden your word in my heart that I might not sin against you."

Hiding God's Word in our hearts is another way of thinking about meditating on Scripture. This means opening ourselves up to the truth of the Word, as though it were a personal word from God to us, and allowing it to become part of us. Our time in the Scriptures can be an immersive experience, where the Word softens our rough edges while also nourishing and growing us. The Word can weave itself into the fabric of who we are as we focus on a passage from the Psalms, the Gospels, or another part of Scripture, and prayerfully ponder it over the course of a day, a week, or even longer. As the Word is stored in our hearts through this repetitive, meditative process and becomes one with us, it will bear fruit not just for the present moment but for the future as well.

How is this kind of fruitfulness possible? One of the ways we foster such transformation is by *speaking* the text. The Hebrew word for "meditation" that we looked at earlier (*hagah*) referred to the process of learning the Bible while pronouncing it aloud, literally murmuring the Word with our mouths. We often refer to this as learning "by heart," but it is more aptly described by the ancients as learning "by mouth."[9] Reading aloud, repeating the words, engages more of our senses and deeply imprints the text upon our minds.[10] In Benedict's sixth-century world, monks did not principally read with their eyes but with their lips, pronouncing what they saw and using their ears to listen to the words they uttered.[11] This form of meditation is also a rich part of Jesus' Jewish heritage.

In addition to adding sound to sight, verbalizing what we read slows down our reading process so we can savor the words like we would if we were reading a poem.[12] This unhurried, leisurely walk through the Word allows the text to trigger associations from other passages, past memories, and connections to our family or work life; stir hope for the future; and make the story of Scripture our story too.[13]

IMAGINING THE STORY

John Chrysostom, the "golden mouthed" preacher of the fourth century, urged his listeners to memorize the Word and then use their imagination to paint portraits of the Scripture on the walls of their minds. In this way, Scripture would become like a room in the art gallery of the mind—a beautiful place, available for continual viewing.[14] The founder of the Jesuits, Ignatius of Loyola, also invites us to exercise our imagination when we read narratives from the Gospels. He suggests reading a Scripture passage two or three times so that the story becomes familiar to us, and then closing our eyes to visualize the setting. Ignatius then invites us to use our five senses of sight, hearing, touch, smell, and taste to imagine ourselves in the story and even to act out the role of one of the characters.[15]

Let's walk through an example of reading the Bible in this way: the story where Jesus walks on water in Matthew 14:22–33. You might begin by imagining the setting. It's two in the morning and you are in a boat on a lake with the disciples when a furious storm breaks out.

What do you hear? What do the waves look like? What is the feeling in your stomach as you bob perilously up and down? How does the wind feel in your face?

In the distance, you see what appears to be a ghost gliding on the water toward you.

How do you feel? How are the others in the boat reacting?

The ghostly apparition gliding toward you on the water speaks in a familiar voice saying, "Take courage! It is I. Don't be afraid."

What emotions do these words stir inside you?

You wonder ... is it the Lord? "Lord, if it's you, tell me to come to you on the water." "Come," Jesus says. You climb out of the boat, and begin to walk on the water toward Jesus.

What is it like to walk on water? How does the churning water feel under your feet? What does Jesus' face look like? What is his expression as he looks at you?

Now, you turn your head and focus on the wind and the waves—and you start to sink.

How cold is the water? What emotions are you experiencing now?

You cry out, "Lord, save me!" Jesus catches you with his hand.

How does his hand feel as it grasps your arm? What is going through your heart? What do you want to say to Jesus now?

Imagining a scene in Scripture helps us become part of the story and allows the story to become part of us.

MEMORIZING SCRIPTURE

Memorizing certain parts of Scripture also enables us to create an inner library that fuels ongoing meditation. William Thierry, a Benedictine monk who lived in the twelfth century, writes in his *Golden Epistle*, "Some part of your reading should, each day, be stored in the stomach of memory enough to be digested. At times it should be brought up again for frequent rumination."[16] Thierry pictures the reading and memorization of Scripture like a cow eating grass, partially digesting it and bringing it up again for further chewing. If you haven't lived on a farm, this may sound rather revolting, but it aptly describes the experience of meditation. Like a cow that works her cud, we can chew on the Word and then come back to it for further nourishment.

If we memorize the Word of God, as Thierry observes, we have the opportunity to access it and to pray it throughout the day.

Benedictine monks took time to memorize Scripture, including all 150 psalms, for their daily office. Today, it is rare to find individuals who have memorized large passages of Scripture. This is especially true because we assume that the Bible will always be accessible to us through the Internet or an electronic device. Yet if we choose to rely solely on this technology we forfeit the gift of being able to internalize the Word and make it part of us. An actor who once played the role of Jesus in a movie memorized, as part of his preparation, all of the recorded words of Jesus in the Gospels. Since that time he has observed, "Whenever I face a dilemma or decision, the words of Jesus come to mind." Meditating on, murmuring, and memorizing the Word give us the freedom to instantly recall it and actually live out what it says.

LIVING THE WORD

The goal of our reading and meditating is to not just *know* God's ways but to *do* God's Word, living in obedience to it. Practicing what we know reinforces the behavior and builds a sound foundation for our lives. The night before he was crucified, Jesus spoke of the importance of putting his words into action: "Now that you know these things, you will be blessed if you do them" (John 13:17).

With the advent of the Internet, we consume far more information than we can possibly put into practice. I recently talked to a young man who attends our Sunday evening service. He shared with me how he had been to two other services earlier in the day (he attends three churches). He also pulled out his mp3 player and showed me the titles of a sermon series by a well-known television preacher he was listening to between the services. Initially, I was impressed by his yearning to learn. But later I wondered, "Is he truly able to ingest and apply all the information he is taking in?" One of the dangers of being contemporary followers of Jesus is the habit of passively storing information without acting on it. If we gorge on Scripture, filling our minds with information but never living it out, we become spiritually fat and sluggish. In some cases, we may even grow immune to the conviction of the Word, hearing it with our minds but never changing the way we live.

Jean Leclercq observes that in the ancient secular usage, *meditari* (to meditate) meant to reflect, but also clearly implied "an intent to *do* it" (emphasis added). Because *meditari* would invariably lead to *action* and not merely remain in the realm of thought, medical doctors in the ancient world actually prescribed meditative reading to their patients who were in need of physical exercise.[17] When we learn something "by heart" by meditating on it, murmuring it with our mouths, fixing it in our memories, and putting it into practice, Scripture becomes more than a bone for us to gnaw on. It becomes food for our souls, food that nourishes our hunger for God.

QUESTIONS FOR REFLECTION AND DISCUSSION

1. A. W. Tozer writes that the ultimate goal of Scripture is a personal encounter with the living God. Do you agree? Has this been your experience?
2. What practices might best help you meditate on Scripture; for example: *lectio divina*, imaging a scene in Scripture, memorizing the Word?
3. Is there a passage of Scripture that might be fruitful for you to memorize? Is there an optimal time when you might be able to commit this text to memory?
4. Is there a Scripture that you are currently being called to live into?

WRITING YOUR RULE

Write down a daily or weekly rhythm for you to feed on the Word (you may find this overlaps with your prayer times).

PART 3
RELATE

— CHAPTER 7 —

FRIENDSHIP: COMPANIONS FOR THE JOURNEY

You may have hundreds, perhaps even thousands of "friends" in your social network, but have you ever experienced true friendship with someone? If you have, you know the difference between an online "friend" and an authentic friendship. In a *New York Times Magazine* article a few years ago, Hal Niedzviecki wrote about the experience of starting his Facebook account. Soon after he joined, Hal had accumulated seven hundred "friends." "I was absurdly proud," he writes, "of how many 'friends'—and even strangers—I'd managed to sign up." But the irony was that while he had more *online* friends, he had fewer *actual* friends to spend time with than ever before. So he decided to have a Facebook party to turn his online friends into actual in-person friends.

Hal invited all seven hundred of his Facebook friends to his favorite local bar. Fifteen of them said they *would* be there, and sixty others said they *might* be there. He guessed that only about twenty people would actually show up. That evening he showered, splashed on some cologne, put on new pants and his favorite shirt, then headed over to the neighborhood watering hole and waited.

And waited.

And waited.

Eventually, one person did show up. It was a woman he didn't even know. She was a friend of a "friend." They ended up making small talk and she left. Hal sat at the bar alone and waited until midnight. Niedzviecki concludes his article with these words: "Seven hundred friends, and I was drinking alone that night."[1]

The Internet makes it easy for us to network and connect with people. Yet, in an ironic twist, North Americans say that they have fewer close friends than ever before. In 1985, only one in ten Americans reported having no close confidants; twenty years later, one in four said they had no close confidants.[2] In his book *Bowling Alone*, Harvard professor Robert Putnam explains how the rise of technologies like the Internet and television have contributed to the decline of informal social activities—dinner parties, bowling leagues, community groups, and the like—that foster friendships.[3] The very technologies designed to link us together end up driving us apart.

This decline in real friendships and the resulting loneliness we experience are not without cost. Medical researchers and social scientists have pointed out that a strong link exists between friendship and well-being. People with close friendships tend to have better health, are more fulfilled, and live longer. The village of Roseto, Pennsylvania, contains a close-knit community of Italian immigrants who frequently stop to chat on the street, visit with one another, and even cook for each other in their backyards. Researchers who have studied this village have shown that people end up living longer if they stay in Roseto than if they move away. This increased health and life expectancy wherever there is a strong sense of community has been coined "the Roseto effect."[4]

Strong friendships also can make a difference in our psychological well-being. In 1937, a researcher at Harvard began a long-range study on the key factors that contribute to human well-being and happiness. The study tracked a group of 268 men who entered Harvard College in the late 1930s over the course of seventy years. The researchers followed them through their life experiences: war, career, marriage, divorce, parenthood, grandparenthood, and old age. One of the things that surprised these ambitious, elite men (now in their nineties) as they looked back over their lives was the fact that it was not their career successes nor their celebrated accomplishments that brought them the greatest satisfaction but their relationships with family and friends.[5]

CREATED FOR RELATIONSHIP

When God created the world—separating the light from darkness, the ground from the seas, and making plants, trees, fish, birds, and mammals—he deemed all that he had made "very good."[6] Then God saw something in his created work that was *not* good and uttered these telling words: "It is not good that man is alone."[7] Keep in mind that Adam had the *ideal* life in Eden: an intimate relationship with God unmarred by sin, a pristine paradise filled with unimaginable wonders. As a farmer and zoologist, Adam had fulfilling work that engaged both his mind and body. He had a limitless supply of delectable food. Yet even with all of these gifts, God says that "it is not good for man to be alone."

We can have a relationship with God, fulfilling work to do, and an enviable home and lifestyle—but if we don't have close friendships with others, we soon realize that something essential is missing. This is because God has made us in his likeness. God is one, yet God exists in a community of three: the Father, the Son, and the Holy Spirit. At the center of the universe is a relationship.[8] Relationships are woven into our nature, crafted into our DNA. When we connect with others in healthy, loving ways, we reflect the image of God.

Life-giving relationships are as important to our spiritual growth and well-being as prayer and Bible reading. They serve an important role in the trellis that supports our life with God. In this chapter, we will look at the importance of spiritual friendship, and in the following two chapters we will examine the crucial connection between our spiritual life and our sexuality and family relationships.

A FRIEND COMMITS

Close friendships immerse us in what Saint Benedict called "a school of service for the Lord." In friendships we have an ideal environment in which to grow the godlike qualities of love and loyalty, perseverance, and courage.[9] The famous friendship of Jonathan and David in the Scriptures offers a particularly poignant example of the way friends can sharpen one another. Jonathan and David ought to have been rivals—both were attractive, athletic, and gifted emerging leaders in Israel. And both of these men were seen as potential heirs to the throne of Jonathan's father, King Saul.

Yet despite the potential for them to be enemies, these two men had a deep friendship based on a promise they had made to one another. In 1 Samuel 18:1–4, we are given a window into the depth of their friendship: "Jonathan became one in spirit with David, and he loved him as himself.... And Jonathan made a covenant with David because he loved him as himself. Jonathan took off the robe he was wearing and gave it to David, along with his tunic, and even his sword, his bow and his belt." Jonathan made his friendship covenant with David even though it would cost him the favor of his father King Saul and the throne itself. In fact, he gave David his robe and sword as a sign of his willingness to relinquish his birthright to the throne. David in turn committed to Jonathan by promising to show unending kindness to Jonathan and his family.[10] David had a true friend in Jonathan—and Jonathan in David—because they willingly made sacrificial commitments to each other.

Aelred of Rievaulx, the twelfth-century Cistercian monk, argues in his classic *Spiritual Friendship*, that the mark of a true friend is the willingness to stand with someone even when it is difficult to do so.[11] A "fair-weather friend" is an oxymoron, a contradiction in terms. Lord Byron once famously remarked, "Friendship is love without wings."[12] Friends will not fly away when we suffer or fail. We know who our true friends are by recalling those who didn't abandon us when we went through difficult circumstances. A real friend, like Christ, stands shoulder to shoulder with us in times of trouble and hardship to make our burden lighter by carrying it with us.

A FRIEND LIFTS YOU UP

While many of us have known the sustaining friendship of a peer, as was true for David and Jonathan, we can also experience the blessing of a friendship with someone of a different generation. Richard Rohr says that every young man needs an older man in his life, not to receive knowledge from him, but to receive his spirit.[13] Likewise, a younger woman needs an older woman, not so much to receive information from her, but to receive her spirit. I have been shaped through friendships with older men and women. Leighton Ford, who led the life-changing pilgrimage to Ireland I mentioned at the beginning of the book, has been a longtime mentor and friend. I first spent time with Leighton as a seminary student in Boston when he asked me to drive him to the home of a friend and board member of his ministry. I picked him up from the airport late one night and invited him to recline his seat and get some sleep. Instead, Leighton crossed his long legs, partially reclined the seat, and said, "I don't think I'll sleep ... tell me your life story." That invitation sparked a friendship and for almost two decades Leighton has been available as an attentive friend on my journey.

In the summer of 1996, when I first came to Tenth Avenue Church in Vancouver where I now serve as pastor, I was intimidated by the challenge of pastoring a historic church whose "glory years" were the 1950s. Church attendance had dwindled from over one thousand to one *hundred* and something, and the church had cycled through almost twenty pastors in twenty years. On one of my first days there, the church secretary walked into my office and said, "If the ship sinks now everyone will blame you because you were the last person at the helm." She was trying to inspire me to work hard, but her words only left me feeling more anxious than ever.

A couple of weeks later, Leighton and I were sitting in my car not far from the church. I felt a desperate need for encouragement but was too ashamed to ask for it. Instead, I asked for some counsel. He paused and said, "Remember that God is an artist; he will not lead you to copy anyone else. Seek God for his unique vision for this place." Through those words—but even more through his generous spirit—I received the strength to walk those first wobbly weeks and months at Tenth. In the presence of a friend, our spirits are lifted and we are encouraged not to despair.

A FRIEND LETS YOU IN

I first learned the word *anamcara* during my pilgrimage to Ireland. *Anam* is the Gaelic word for "soul," *cara* the word for "friend." An *anamcara* is a "soul friend." Originally, this referred to someone to whom you confessed your secrets and sins, but it later came to mean someone with whom you could share your innermost self, your mind and heart.[14] Aelred describes this kind of spiritual friend as one with whom we can share "all our confidences and plans."[15] We need a friend in whose presence we can be completely open and transparent, a soul friend with whom we can *relax our heart*.[16] As Thomas Merton has observed, the soul is shy—like a wild animal. It flees from noise and takes cover in the underbrush. Only in a place of safety will it surface again.[17] When we feel safe and understood, our souls surface and we open up to others. We shed the half-truths and the facades and share our secrets, dreams, fears, failures, and hopes.

It's important to know who your friends are. You may have many "friends" who are really just acquaintances. Aelred says that we may care for these people, but "it would be imprudent to lay bare our souls and pour out our inner hearts to them."[18] We should "bare our souls" only to those we are certain want the best for us, know us better than most, and would never betray us. We should "not form intimacies too quickly."[19] Soul friends take time to cultivate, and we will likely only have one or two at most at any given time of life. Again, Aelred writes, "But what happiness, what security, what joy to have someone to whom you dare to speak on terms of equality as to another self; one to whom you need have no fear to confess your failings; one to whom you can unblushingly make known what progress we have made in the spiritual life; one to whom you can entrust all the secrets of your heart and before whom you can place all your plans!"[20] Having a trusted friend to share our stories, anxieties, joys, burdens, struggles, and hopes is a priceless gift. We feel lighter and freer. But spiritual friendship is not just something that makes us *feel* better; it's a gift that helps us *become* better. The goal of a spiritual friendship is not to have all of our viewpoints validated but to be formed in Christ. A true friend offers encouragement but is also willing to challenge and even rebuke us.

A FRIEND SPEAKS THE HARD TRUTH

My friend Elizabeth was a nationally ranked javelin thrower in college. As an undergraduate she would sometimes walk around the Stanford campus with her javelin perched on her shoulder—even when she wasn't headed to track practice. Elizabeth also carries a "javelin" with her in her personal relationships: the ability to speak well-aimed, incisive truths that her friends need to hear. Not only does Elizabeth see and name good things in me that I don't see clearly or have forgotten, she just as regularly points out rough edges such as my tendency toward workaholism. After the birth of my son, she urged me to spend more time at home with my wife and him. I remember her saying to me, "Others can travel and speak, but no one else can be a husband to Sakiko and a father to Joey." When she sensed that I was slipping into a place of unhealthy emotional vulnerability with someone, she charged me to make sure I had appropriate boundaries in place. The book of Proverbs tells us the wounds of a friend are better than the kisses of any enemy. I am blessed to be wounded by a friend as candid as Elizabeth.

No one has a 360-degree perspective on their life. Just as there is a blind spot in the retina of the eye, there is also a blind spot in the soul where we cannot see the truth about ourselves.[21] A spiritual friend will identify our blind spot with love, but they *will* identify it. If they see us walking down a path of over- (or under-) committing to work, making poor financial choices, or placing ourselves in a compromising relationship, they will care for us by *naming* these things. A true friend will name the attitudes and actions that are causing us to drift *from* God even as they actively point us *to* God.

PRACTICES THAT SUPPORT SPIRITUAL FRIENDSHIP

The purpose of spiritual friendship is to grow in our love for Christ. Spiritual friendship is *"life in and with Christ,* and *life for the sake of Christ"* (emphasis added).[22] My friend Mike has experienced this in his twenty-year friendship with Brandon. Mike and Brandon met as teenagers and soon became drinking buddies hanging out at night-clubs. When they became young adults, each of them individually made choices to deepen their commitment to Christ and move away from their partying lifestyles. As their life with God grew, their friendship was transformed and they began to encourage each other in their spiritual journeys. They now live in different communities (about an hour's drive from each other), but they are deliberate about spending time together. Mike explains, "We've committed to pray-ing for each other every day and try to connect by phone at least once a week. We also send emails, text messages, and Facebook posts that encourage, support, and make us laugh—we laugh a lot. We also take about one night per month to get together in person to pray, talk, and do something fun—like attend a concert, go camping, or we'll just go to each other's houses and hang with our wives and kids." It's hard to overestimate how the presence of a fellow pilgrim in our lives can keep us walking in the way of Christ.

Because spiritual friendships help us grow in our love for Christ they are a vital spiritual discipline, yet they do not exist in isolation from other elements of our rule of life. Several other practices within our rule directly support our relationships.

PLAY

Part of the way Mike and Brandon connect is by playing together. For many men the best way to connect with another guy is by doing some-thing they both enjoy. I find it feels more natural for me to spend time with certain men when we run, bike, or sail rather than just having "coffee" together and talking. As we will see in a later chapter, playing together draws us closer to other people. This is why people who want to get to know a potential romantic partner will invite them to go on a date which typically involves play—seeing a movie, sharing a meal, or rollerblading. This is also why those of us who are married and want to deepen our friendship with our spouse will continue to engage in these kinds of activities with them. Playing with someone is an organic way to initiate and deepen a relationship.

FACE-TO-FACE CONTACT

William Deresiewicz writes: "Having recently moved across the country, I thought that Facebook would help me feel connected to the friends I'd left behind. But now I find the opposite is true. Reading about the mundane details of their lives, a steady stream of trivia and ephemera, leaves me feeling both empty and unpleasantly full, as if I had just binged on junk food, and precisely because it reminds me of the real sustenance, the real knowledge, we exchange by email or phone or face-to-face."[23] Social media can easily become the equivalent of junk food for our soul. While it allows us to share photos with siblings and friends who live in distant places, we can also get caught up in the mundane details of other people's lives. This can offer us a false sense of intimacy, detached from any face-to-face contact with real people. Spend time with real people and don't settle for the substitute of virtual relationships.

SERVICE

Serving alongside others also provides a natural way to grow friendships. In a Benedictine monastery every monk, including the abbot, participates in kitchen chores. This shared service engenders humility among the brothers, helps to diminish the pecking order, and creates a way for the monks to build relationships.

Our church is situated in a beautiful but lonely city. People often tell me, "It's hard to meet people here [let alone make friends]." Vancouver has a high percentage of college and university students, serves as a gateway city for immigrants from Asia to the rest of North America, and has a highly transient population. At our church, we encourage people to serve (among other reasons) as a way to get to know other people. Cutting carrots and tomatoes alongside others as you prepare a meal for homeless people, or hammering a nail into a home that you and fellow volunteers are building for an impoverished family not only blesses those you are serving but also can begin or deepen friendships.

PRAYER

Penny and Allison meet for a long walk along False Creek each week. They begin by talking to each other but often naturally speak with

God as well. This may sound strange to you, but if we believe Christ is in our midst it makes sense. In Scripture, we are assured that where two of God's children (or more) are gathered, Christ is present (Matthew 18:20) in a special way. Praying with and for our *anamcara* deepens our spiritual friendship with them. Aelred says to his friend Ivo, "Here we are, you and I, and I hope a third, Christ, is in our midst."[24]

My friend Gordon Smith once shared with me that one of the most formative experiences of his spiritual life was meeting every three weeks with his friend Darrell over lunch. Each time they came together, they asked each other, "Since we met last, what have been your joys and sorrows?" Using Ignatius's prayer of *Examen*, they shared where they were feeling joy, a sense of being alive, connection with God (what Ignatius described as *consolation*), and where they were experiencing sadness, anger, or a sense of distance from God (what Ignatius called *desolation*). As Gordon and Darrell used this ancient form of prayer, they grew more transparent with one another and in their friendship with Christ.

FINDING A SPIRITUAL FRIEND

If you do not yet have a true spiritual friend, how can you go about seeking one?

First of all, pray that God would give you a friend. In Scripture, we see repeatedly how God orchestrates the coming together of friends: David and Jonathan, Ruth and Naomi, Paul and Barnabas, and, of course, Jesus and his disciples. Our friends are gifts from God, and we can pray that God would fulfill his plan and draw us into the friendships he has ordained for us.

Secondly, ask people to do things with you and initiate opportunities to deepen your relationship. The fact that God offers the gift of friendship with others doesn't mean we don't participate in the process. Being intentional can make a difference. Sometimes, all that keeps two people from entering into a spiritual friendship is an initial conversation. Don't be afraid to invite someone to meet once or twice to share each other's stories and discern if a mutual sense of purpose and connection exists. After having met, if you both have a sense of peace and freedom from God, you might establish a rhythm of meeting together (or talking by phone together, if you live far away from each other) for six months or a year. After that time, give each other the space and permission to evaluate whether it would be fruitful to continue meeting. As we've seen, a rule of life isn't about trying to cram more into our already crowded lives. It's about saying no to certain things in order to say yes to others. It's about giving each part of our lives the time it deserves. Friendships take time, sweat, and sacrifice; they can lead to disappointment, frustration, and even heartbreak. But they are worth it. Jesus had about one thousand days to "save the world," and though he knew all twelve of his closest students would bail on him and two would betray him, he spent most of that time with this group. Over three and a half years, they became his friends.

Finally, be a friend to others. The best way to grow a friendship, of course, is to be a friend. People who genuinely show friendship are precious and increasingly rare. We live in a time when our "friends," as someone has put it, are "little dehydrated packets of images and information, no more my [real] friends than a set of baseball cards is the New York Mets."[25] Decide to swim against the current of our culture and form true friendships in which you commit to others, lift them up, and let them into your life. You can cultivate *anamcaras* as you speak the hard truth in love and point people to God. This kind of friendship will not happen simply through our own efforts; it is a gift that we receive from God through our deepening friendship with him. In the upper room before going to the cross Jesus said, "I no longer call you servants, because a servant does not know his master's business. Instead, I have called you friends, for everything that I learned from my Father I have made known to you."[26] As our rule of life helps us deepen our friendship with Jesus, we in turn can offer true friendship to others.

QUESTIONS FOR REFLECTION
AND DISCUSSION

1. How does the Internet help friendships? How does the Internet hinder friendships?
2. In what ways do friendships foster our overall well-being?
3. Do you agree that life-giving friendships are just as important as prayer or reading the Bible to our spiritual flourishing?
4. What characteristics of David and Jonathan's friendship struck you most deeply in this chapter? What other friendships—biblical or otherwise—have inspired or instructed you?
5. What are your greatest fears in friendship? What are your greatest hopes?

WRITING YOUR RULE

If you can think of a potential spiritual friend, jot down his or her name and how you might initiate an ongoing relationship. If you already have such a friend in your life, draft a rhythm of when you might meet and future topics you would enjoy discussing.

— CHAPTER 8 —

SEX AND SPIRITUALITY

A few years ago, I was on a sailing trip along British Columbia's beautiful Sunshine Coast. The weather was spectacular, the azure blue sky and sunlight bringing the rugged shoreline into sharp focus. In the evening we sailed into a quiet cove and the setting sun turned our inlet into a pool of gold. As night began to descend, stars appeared like countless holes in the floor of heaven. I thought I had died and gone to paradise. It was almost perfect. There was just one thing missing: my wife Sakiko. She was at home hosting a friend from Japan, and I longed for her to stand beside me and revel in this grandeur.

Can you recall a soaring moment of your life? If you happened to be alone, chances are you wish you could have shared that experience with a friend or family member. Because we are made in the image of a relational God, we feel a desire to connect with other human beings. Our longing to connect with other people in a way that brings life is an expression of our God-given sexuality. Our sexuality involves far more than just the act of sexual intercourse. The Greek word *eros* (from which we get the word *erotic*) can mean a desire for sex itself, but in the original sense of the word, *eros* refers to a natural desire for beauty or a longing for relational intimacy. Likewise, the biblical understanding of human sexuality is much broader than the act of sex itself. For example, when we are at a family gathering and realize with a bit of surprise perhaps, "I actually like these people" (well, almost all of them!) we are expressing our desire for relational intimacy—which is an expression of our sexuality. *Eros*, understood in this broader sense, can also refer to the awe that we feel when we stand with a good friend at Niagara Falls and feel the spray on our faces; or the euphoria and solidarity Canadians feel with each other when their hockey team wins the Olympic gold.[1]

I believe that this broader, ancient understanding of our sexuality is particularly helpful today. We live in a time when more people than ever before are single. Many people for a variety of reasons are not able to engage in sexual intercourse or have an aversion to sex because of a painful or disappointing experience in their past. A surprising number of young people inspired by new monastic communities are choosing to remain unmarried and chaste so they are freer to offer more of themselves to God and others. The wider definition of *eros* acknowledges that whether we are having sex or not, we are sexual beings and that our sexual energy profoundly shapes our lives.

Our sexual energy, as Ronald Rolheiser says in *Holy Longing*, is the most powerful of all fires, the best of all fires, and the most dangerous of all fires.[2] It can lead us to ecstasy or despair, to heaven or hell. A fire set in a fireplace can warm the entire house, but a fire set to the curtains can burn it down. A healthy rule of life that guides and directs our sexuality will not repress our sexual energy but help us to channel it so that we can more deeply connect with other people and bring them life. A rule of life around our sexuality is not a dam that blocks the flow of our sexual energy; it is more like the banks of a river, helping to direct a powerful current. A rule of life provides helpful boundaries that guide and channel our sexuality toward things that are life-giving and honor God's created purposes.

Our culture is naive about the power of sex. People speak of casual sex. They describe a sexual encounter as "no big deal." Young people talk about "hooking up" in a way that is free of romance or any relational commitment. In contrast to this cultural understanding of "casual" sex, God tells us that sex is powerfully bonding. God created sex as a unitive act that makes two people one, body and soul. In Genesis 2:24, we read that when a man and a woman unite in sex the *two become one flesh*. God designed sex so that when a man and a woman come together physically in sexual union, a force is at work that makes them naturally want to unite on every other level as well: emotionally, spiritually, and even economically. It is an act of connection so sublime that it is even used in Scripture as a metaphor to describe our union with God.

If this understanding of the power of sex sounds ethereal or otherworldly, consider the opinion of Dr. Gordon Neufeld, a respected secular psychologist. In his best-selling book, *Hold On to Your Kids*, he writes:

> Sex is a potent bonding agent: It creates couples, attaches to each other those who engage in it. Studies have confirmed what most of us will have found out on our own, that making love has a natural bonding effect, evoking powerful emotions of attachment in the human brain.... Simply put, sex creates a potent connection and then harnesses the rest of the brain through chemicals the brain releases to preserve the bond that has been created.... Sex creates couples, ready or not, willing or not.... Sex is like human contact cement, invoking a sense of union and fusion, creating one flesh.[3]

If sex does in fact make two people one, it makes sense that in the safety of a committed, loving marriage covenant, sex will lead to joy, delight, and even powerful healing. But when sex is used outside of God's design, it gradually loses its potency as a bonding agent and lessens our capacity to experience true sexual intimacy and lasting fulfillment.

The Bible also warns us to avoid sex outside of a covenant relationship because the power of sex can make us enslaved or addicted to it. In 1 Corinthians 6:12, Paul, echoing a famous Corinthian saying, writes, "I have the right to do anything, but not everything is beneficial ... I will not be mastered by anything." He then calls us to avoid sexual immorality[4] citing the language of Genesis 2:24, "[The two] will become one flesh." Paul recognized that engaging in sexual activity outside of a covenant relationship may *momentarily* satisfy our hunger, but it doesn't fulfill it in a lasting way. This is why so-called casual sex or viewing pornography can be so addictive and undermine our capacity for healthy, long-term relationships. Like using drugs, when people engage in sexual activity apart from God's will, they find themselves craving more and more of what satisfies less and less. They become trapped in an addiction cycle.[5]

What does it look like to foster a healthy sexuality so that it becomes a part of the trellis that supports our life with God? If expressing our God-given sexuality in ways that honor him and bring life to others is an important part of a vibrant spiritual life, how can we craft a rule of life around our sexual desires? To be clear, we need to recognize that a rule of life does not involve repressing or toning down our sexual energy. Instead, our rule will help us to channel our desires in ways that bring satisfaction, help connect us with others, and bring life to our relationships. Because God designed our sexuality, an essential part of our rule will involve setting healthy boundaries that free us to honor him and his good design for us.

LIFE-GIVING BOUNDARIES

In the years before I was married and called to be a pastor, I was on a trip and met a woman who worked as a model. We were from very different worlds—but we experienced a dynamic chemistry when we first met. At the time, she was in a relationship with someone else, and I was interested in someone back home—so having a fling, though compellingly attractive, wasn't right. One night she showed up at my hotel lobby around midnight. Over the phone, she mentioned that she wanted to come up to my room to show me some of her modeling photographs. Frankly, I wasn't sure that I could trust her ... or myself for that matter. But I also felt excited, attracted to the unknown possibilities that might unfold. In the end, though we talked on the phone for a while, she did not come up to my room. Nothing happened.

After the trip I shared the story with a close friend of mine. He said, "If you are ever in such a situation again, call me." I knew he was right to say this to me. Though I had averted a temptation that could have had disastrous consequences, much of the reason for my struggle was the simple fact that I was alone and isolated while traveling, and I had no one to hold me accountable.

Though it can be embarrassing to share a sexual temptation with another person, one of the best ways to protect ourselves from falling into temptation is to find a friend to whom we can confess our struggles and who will commit to pray for us. All of us will find ourselves in circumstances where the air gets thin and we lose our perspective. One of the best ways to regain it is to have someone who will speak the truth to us. That's part of the reason we need close friends who will hold us accountable.

Setting boundaries is also important when you are involved in a dating relationship. In her book *Real Sex: The Naked Truth about Chastity*, Lauren Winner shares some practical counsel when drawing healthy sexual boundaries as a single person. Winner had been sexually active as a young adult before coming to Christ, and her journey with Christ eventually led her to embrace sexual purity. When she began writing a book on sex, she was a single woman, but during the time she was writing she started dating a man named Griff and they ended up getting married. In her book she describes how she and Griff would regularly take evening walks on the lawn of the University of Virginia near the dome-shaped rotunda. Griff's friend Greg, the campus pastor at the University of Virginia, gave them this helpful piece of guidance as they initially sought to set boundaries for expressing their attraction to one another: "Don't do anything sexual that you wouldn't feel comfortable doing on the steps of the rotunda." As Winner relates: "Griff and I took Greg's words to heart, and even climbed up on to the rotunda steps one night and kissed to our heart's content. Griff said, 'That's it. That's our line. We won't really feel very comfortable stripping our clothes off up here in front of the rotunda.' And that became our mantra on the steps of the rotunda."[6]

Before you find yourself in the heat of a passionate moment, it is a good idea to discuss your vulnerabilities and your commitments with a trusted friend, spiritual advisor, or mentor. Having a friend who shares your values, or a pastor or spiritual director who can give you counsel, will help you walk through the temptations you will face *before* you face them.

HONORING MARRIAGE

Married people also need to craft careful boundaries to protect their sexuality. In a marriage relationship, boundaries can shift slowly, sometimes in ways that are barely perceptible to those involved. A prominent politician who was regarded as a potential presidential candidate for his party made the following confession about an extramarital affair: "I developed a relationship with [someone who] started out as a dear friend.... It began very innocently.... But, recently over this last year, it developed into something much more than that. And as a consequence ... I hurt my wife. I hurt my boys, I hurt you." Like this politician, many people who have had an affair look back and say, "It began very innocently ... we were just friends."

Have you ever found yourself thinking about someone else and wondering, "Does she (or he) find me attractive?" Or you found yourself hoping to run into that person or making excuses to call or get together with them. Or perhaps you've begun to confide your inmost thoughts to this person—your stresses and worries, your hopes and dreams, even some things you have not shared with your spouse—and you sense you've crossed a line. Fifty percent of first-time adulterous relationships happen with friends, people with whom we develop intimate emotional ties before it ever becomes a physical relationship.[7]

In her book *Not "Just Friends"*, Dr. Shirley Glass says that one way to determine whether a particular friendship is threatening to your marriage is to ask, *Where are the walls, and where are the windows?* In a healthy committed relationship, Glass says, a couple constructs a wall that shields them from any outside forces that have the power to split them. They look at the world outside their relationship through a shared window of openness and honesty. The couple is a unit: they have a united front to deal with children, in-laws, and friends.

An affair splits a couple's union. It hoists an interior *wall of secrecy* between the marriage partners, and at the same time it opens a *window of intimacy* between the affair partners. The couple is no longer a unit. The affair partner is on the *inside*, and the marital partner is on the *outside*. Asking ourselves about the placement of walls and windows can help those of us who are married determine when an outside relationship has moved beyond friendship into the zone of an extramarital emotional affair. "If a friend knows more about our marriage than our spouse knows about your friendship, then we have already reversed the healthy position of walls and windows."[8] A healthy rule for a married person is to not become more open and intimate with someone than we are with our own spouse.

PORNOGRAPHY

Increasingly, pornography is considered a socially acceptable form of entertainment. Jesus, however, clearly condemned the kind of lust pornography stimulates (Matthew 5:27–30). Like all sexual activity outside of God's intention, viewing pornography provides a momentary lift, but it leaves a person emptier than before. As social critic Naomi Wolf has pointed out, ironically pornography deadens sexual desire in relation to real people. "For most of human history," she notes, "erotic images have been reflections and celebrations of real naked women. Now for the first time the power of the erotic images supplants those of real women." Wolf says, "Today real naked women are just bad porn."[9] Pornography hurts people. As a pastor, I've observed that when a person in a relationship uses pornography, their partner experiences the same feelings of rejection and betrayal as a victim of an affair.

To cultivate a healthy spirituality through your rule of life you may need to create boundaries to channel your sexual desires away from things that will diminish and destroy you. Practically, you can install software like Covenant Eyes or download resources at xxxchurch.com that will help hold you accountable when you are alone on your computer. You can talk to people and confess your struggle to them. I know someone who speed-dials a trusted friend or two when tempted by pornography. I know others who ask a friend to call them when they are away on a business trip or home alone for an extended period of time. Knowing they are going to be asked about how they dealt with their temptation can make a significant difference in helping them overcome it. I have another friend who has decided not to have a computer or a television in his apartment so that he will not be tempted to view pornography. If that sounds drastic, recall that in the Sermon on the Mount Jesus urged those struggling with lust to take drastic measures.[10]

Remember, appropriate boundaries are important, allowing us to channel our *eros* in ways that honor God and bring life to people.

GIVING LIFE TO OTHERS

G. K. Chesterton once quipped, "Every man who knocks on the door of a brothel is looking for God."[11] If our connection with God has been severed or compromised, we will be more likely to look for intimacy in unhealthy ways, seeking some kind of substitute for the eternal embrace each of us longs for. Conversely, as we enjoy our relationship with God, we will find we are able to love others with greater integrity, less selfishly, and more freely. If we find ourselves overwhelmed with a constant desire for sexual intimacy, something may be missing from our spiritual life. Unbridled sensuality is often a symptom of deeper longings—the longing to be known, valued, and accepted with a kind of love that only God can give. And rather than merely sublimate our sexual desires, our relationship with God heals them and reorders all of our priorities.[12] A healthy sexuality is inseparable from a life-giving friendship with God.

Fostering a healthy rhythm of life around sexuality will include a healthy connection and intimacy with friends. I have a friend I'll call Ray. Ray is single. One day he was feeling sexually restless. He felt like going to a bar, picking up a woman, and having a one-night stand. Although Ray was playing out this scenario in his mind, as a follower of Christ, he was not intending to act it out. Instead he decided to attend a dinner party with some friends. "We had good conversation, good food, and good wine, and through the richness of that experience the sexual temptation was gone." Rather than seek fulfillment of his desires in a destructive way, Ray was unconsciously choosing to express his sexuality—his longing to connect—by relating to his friends.

Healthy connections with others—whether through conversation with friends over a meal, shared laughter, affirming words, or affectionate touch—can make us less vulnerable to unwise sexual pursuits. Likewise, one of the best things a married couple can do to honor and protect their marriage is to foster not only their physical intimacy but also a growing, life-giving friendship with each other. A growing friendship with our spouse will also typically lead to a more meaningful sexual connection. According to psychologist Dr. John Gottman, when a spouse has an affair, the underlying reason is often not primarily sexual.[13] Most spouses are simply seeking understanding, validation, or love. Part of the reason why people engage in sex outside of marriage, turn to porn, or engage in compulsive masturbation is because they have a deeper craving for intimacy and connection. If our souls are content and grateful, we are less likely to succumb to these behaviors that ironically leave our souls emptier.

As we mature as sexual beings, we will also want to create "new life" in people, as we offer them our love and blessing. Kathleen Norris, a writer and poet who spent nearly three years living at a Benedictine monastery in Minnesota, describes how her experience of getting to know actual monks confounded her stereotypes of them as asexual and cold individuals. She found that many people who are involved in religious orders consciously channel their sexual energies so they can love people around them more fully.[14] In her book *The Cloister Walk*, Norris describes her friendship with a celibate priest she calls Tom. His capacity to listen and understand her inspired her to dive into several old, half-finished poems she had started writing and bring them to fruition. "Appreciating Tom's presence in my life as a miraculous, unmerited gift helped me to place our relationship in its proper religious context," she writes, "and also to understand why it was that when I'd seek him out to pray with me, I'd always leave feeling so much better than when I came.... This was celibacy at its best, a man's sexual energies so devoted to the care of others that a few words could lift me out of despair, and give me the strength to reclaim my life."[15]

During her high school years, my younger sister Hana was frequently sought out by girls and boys at her school in Montreal. Attractive and part of the popular "in" crowd, she loved to go to parties and dance. Her chic wardrobe led to her being voted the best dressed person in her graduating class. Today, she works as a high school guidance counselor and teacher. At lunch time, rather than eating with her fellow teachers, she spends time with students, many of whom lack friends and would otherwise eat alone. Instead, they come to her office and have lunch with her. In her presence, they started to blossom in small ways: edging out of their shell, making a little more eye contact, smiling.

Several years ago I was spending time with a boy named Ethan, then ten. One afternoon when I was at his house, I saw that he had a football in the garage and picked it up. "Do you like football?" I asked. "I really don't know how to play football," Ethan replied. (One of the reasons he may not have known how to play football was that his dad died when he was a younger boy.) It had been a long time since I had played football, but I grabbed the ball and showed Ethan how to spread his fingers across the laces, cock the ball behind his ear, and release it. We spent part of the afternoon throwing the football back and forth. A few weeks later, his mom told me about his newfound obsession: Ethan took the ball wherever he went—including tagging along with his mother on a grocery store errand. He would repeatedly exclaim, "Mom, this is how you throw a ball!" I would not have thought in these terms then, but teaching Ethan how to throw a football was an expression of my desire to create and impart life.

When we connect with others in ways that bring life, whether it involves inspiring someone to write a poem, welcoming them in a way that instills confidence, or teaching them how to throw a football, we are expressing our sexuality, our desire to give and nurture life.

As we have seen, a rule of life isn't just about saying no for the sake of saying no, but saying no to some things in order to say a greater yes. For example, a pilgrim of Christ may voluntarily abstain from food for a time in order to say a fuller yes to God. In the past when I have fasted, my mind has felt clearer and my spirit more sensitive to God (though sometimes, I've simply been grumpier!). Through fasting, a new world opens up to me. If you can't eat because you don't have money to buy food and are starving, you will feel devastated and deprived of life. But if you don't eat because you *choose* not to eat as a way to attend more fully to God, then, as hard as that is, it can be a life-giving experience.

Choosing a path of sexual purity—a married person committing to reserve sex for marriage or a single person choosing to abstain from sexual intercourse—is a radical practice in our world today. Like fasting, it is a countercultural way of saying yes to God, yes to being able to give ourselves more wholly to others, and yes to ourselves and our wholeness. Monks and nuns make a very particular sexual vow to God: to remain single and sexually chaste. This commitment baffles some people who fail to understand their underlying motives. Those who voluntarily choose the path of celibacy are typically not saying no to sex for the sole sake of self-denial but in order to say yes in a fuller way to God and to serving and loving other people. By remaining single and sexually chaste, they create a holy vacancy for God. The beloved priest Henri Nouwen says of this call to singleness, "We become empty for God, free, and open for his presence and available for his service."[16] A single person who commits to sexual chastity has a unique space for God and for others.

Several years ago while in Manila, I had the opportunity to meet Thomas Green, a Jesuit priest who wrote perceptively on the spiritual life. We sat together in an outdoor square at the university, where he taught philosophy and theology. Mustering some courage, I asked him about his call to the priesthood and celibacy. He said something like this: "I grew up in a happy home with loving parents and brothers and sisters. I thought no gift could be greater than being married and having a family of my own. But, as a young man, I wanted to offer Jesus something precious. As I thought and prayed about it, I felt like I wanted to offer Jesus my right to be married and have children. Let me explain. If you were in my office and I were to hand you a piece of art saying, 'I don't like this. I want to get rid of it, here please take it,' that wouldn't honor you. But, if I were to hand you a piece of art saying, 'This is my favorite, something that I consider priceless,' I would honor you."

When single people offer up their right to have sex for a season or for the rest of their lives, or when married people offer up their option to pursue sex outside of their marriage by being faithful to their spouse, they offer an infinitely precious gift to Jesus. They also offer a gift to themselves as they find they become more deeply connected to God, themselves, and have more of their whole selves to offer others.

REVIRGINIZATION

As you have read this chapter, you may have had a bittersweet reaction. Perhaps you feel that you have fallen short or have been compromised because of your past experiences, failing to live out God's ideal within his boundaries for expressing your sexuality in healthy ways. Perhaps your sexual purity feels like a ship that sailed away long ago.

The good news is that with God there is always hope for a new beginning.

Priest Ronald Rolheiser describes how he received a confession from a woman whom he describes as being sophisticated, very sexually experienced, and deeply unhappy. "There was not a childlike bone in her body," he writes. "She had lost most of her virginity." After this confession, as a pastor he offered her this prescription: "revirginization."[17] He shared with her that forests can be destroyed by pollution or by fire, as was the case some years ago at Yellowstone National Park. Sometimes only dirty, black soot remains. However, as was true at Yellowstone, given enough time—the rains will come, the sun will shine, and vegetation will slowly reemerge. The flowers come back, the trees begin to grow, the beauty returns, and in a manner of speaking, the forest *revirginizes*.

The same is true for us. By the grace of God we can revirginize, reexperiencing God's ideal of purity through the forgiveness of Christ. In Ezekiel 36:25–27 we read these words of hope: "I will sprinkle clean water on you, and you will be clean; I will cleanse you from all your impurities and from all your idols. I will give you a new heart and put a new spirit in you; I will remove from you your heart of stone and give you a heart of flesh. And I will put my Spirit in you and move you to follow my decrees and be careful to keep my laws." You may struggle with an ongoing sense of regret or shame over past sexual sins, but God promises to sprinkle clean water on you and make you clean. He offers you a new heart. You don't need to be defined by your past. When you turn to God, you experience a new beginning.

Weaving a healthy sexuality into the tapestry of a healthy rule of life is no easy matter. It will not be the result of a last-minute decision or tacked on as an afterthought. It will require us to swim against the tide of the culture, thinking about healthy boundaries, seeking friends who share Christ's values, and relying on the power of the Holy Spirit to channel our sexual energy in ways that honor God, ourselves, and other people. In the end, we will find this is the way to experience the fullness of our sexuality and know the joy of imparting this life-giving gift to others.

QUESTIONS FOR REFLECTION AND DISCUSSION

1. How did you respond to the broader definition of sexuality presented in this chapter?
2. Why is the expression "casual sex" a contradiction in terms?
3. Think of someone you know who has healthy sexual boundaries. What do those boundaries consist of?
4. Why is good friendship such an important part of cultivating a healthy sexuality?
5. Whether we are single or married, what are some healthy nongenital ways to express our sexuality?
6. How can we say yes to God through our sexuality?
7. What hope can a person who feels sexually compromised find in God?

WRITING YOUR RULE

As you reflect on your rule, what practical boundaries would help you foster sexual purity? Take a moment to write them here and discuss them with someone you trust.

— CHAPTER 9 —

FAMILY TIES

Our rule of life is best lived out in what Saint Benedict referred to as a "school of love"—a community where we learn firsthand to offer and receive care. For most of us, this involves the immediate members of our household, the people who have a front-row seat in our lives. They see our faults and inconsistencies, our self-flattery, our self-deception. For this reason, our family relationships are a powerful crucible God uses to refine our character.

I know this has been true in my own life. When I was single, I traveled an average of once a month for a speaking engagement or a ministry-related commitment. That pace altered slightly when I got married, but it didn't change significantly. Then along came Joey, our son. Just six weeks after his birth, I went on a weeklong ministry trip to Mexico City where I met with a small group of young emerging leaders who had gathered from different parts of the world. My wife pleaded with me not to go, but at the time I felt like my role as the mentor to this group made my presence essential (and I was too embarrassed to flake out a few weeks beforehand). I quietly hoped that Joey's sleep habits would magically improve in his seventh week. Instead, they tanked. He screamed through entire nights. It was one of the hardest weeks of Sakiko's life.

When I returned, my wife and I had a long, tense conversation. It was more of a monologue—and I wasn't the one preaching. After this unforgettable sermon from my wife, I canceled my work-related travel for the next year so I could spend more time at home. I set new boundaries for my work schedule, and committed to being home

each day at 5:15 p.m. If you have young children, you know that
the hour before dinner can be one of the hardest hours of the day.
I also set new guidelines so I was around more in the evenings. I
decided that I would not dedicate more than three nights per week to
my work. Though there are sometimes exceptions to this rule (rules
must be flexible), they are rare.

I admit I sometimes feel conflicted by these boundaries. Some
of the pastors I went to school with are now on the speaking cir-
cuit, pursuing national ministries, and traveling around the world.
There's a part of me that loves that kind of life. But I also know that
no one else can be a husband to my wife and a father to my son.
I feel peace with my rule of life, knowing that the deepest part of
me wants to stay and be present with my family. I want to be here,
involved in what God is doing in my local community. It may not be
glamorous, but here's a little secret: I'm discovering that family life is
more fulfilling than trying to climb the ladder of achievement. Each
January, I look back across the past twelve months and jot down the
things for which I am most grateful. Without hesitating, I place my
wife Sakiko and our son Joey at the top of my list.

THE FURNACE OF THE FAMILY

With all their joys and frustrations, families are the ideal place for
faith to grow. When the heat gets turned up in the furnace of our
household and we experience challenges with our parents, a sibling,
a spouse, our children, or our housemates, a part of us wants to pivot
and run. But when we run from our family we avoid one of the most
effective ways God uses to shape and refine our character.

We may imagine that monks and nuns lead lives of heavenly
peace in idyllic communities, free from the daily conflict, tension,
and relational problems that plague our families. But our cloistered
brothers and sisters will testify that friction with roommates and
other members of the order is frequent—and often necessary. They
see these relational challenges as one of the primary means that God
uses to refine them.[1] Single priest Ronald Rolheiser says life in a fam-

ily (or another form of intentional familial community) "humbles us, deflates our ego, puts us into purgatory and then into heaven."[2]

This raises the question: why *does* God place us in families? What is the purpose of these relationships? Author Gary Thomas raises an interesting question here when he asks: "What if God designed family more to make us holy, more than to make us happy?" In other words, what if the primary purpose of our family is to purify us into the people God wants us to become, not to have all of our immediate felt needs met? What if God designed family both as a community of joy *and* as a furnace to shrink our selfishness, draw us closer to Jesus, and help us to live and love well?[3]

A RULE OF LIFE IN THE CONTEXT OF OUR FAMILY

I have found various elements of a rule of life to be especially relevant to life in a family or household. As you build your own rule, prayerfully consider if one or two of these resonate with you and could serve as a starting (or restarting) point for you and your family.

UNITING FOR REST AND WORSHIP

Most families are not conscious of having a rule of life, but all families have routines that shape their life together. One of the simplest rhythms to develop is the pattern of a weekly Sabbath that includes participation in a local church. Worship in community honors our Maker's good design for our families. Households that regularly participate in a worshiping community experience a variety of benefits. For example, children who participate in church face significantly lower incidents of drug and alcohol abuse, depression, and suicide than children who do not.[4]

While there are other activities families can participate in together, from playing in a soccer league to skiing on the weekend, something about the experience of being together with others in worship each week is vital in keeping us and our loved ones close to God.

This is more than merely a theoretical point. An athletic trainer I know, Lisa, works with elite NCAA Division I athletes and finds that the subject of faith sometimes comes up in conversation. When Lisa asks these students if they were ever involved in church, almost all of them look at her wistfully and say, "I used to go all the time, then I joined a traveling soccer (basketball or softball) team during elementary school and my parents and I stopped going. I've never gone back."

If our weekends become so consumed with sports and recreation that our participation in community worship is marginalized, we need to ask ourselves, "What is our *main* priority?"

Stephen Covey in *First Things First* talks about priorities by sharing this story:

> One day a teacher set a one-gallon, wide-mouthed jar on the table at the front of the classroom. He produced a platter of about a dozen fist-sized rocks and placed them one at a time into the jar. When the jar was filled to the top and no more rocks would fit inside, he asked, "Is this jar full?" Everyone in the class said, "Yes."
>
> Then he reached under the table and pulled out a bucket of gravel. He dumped some gravel into the jar and shook it, causing it to work down into the spaces between the big rocks. He asked the students again, "Is the jar full now?" Aware that this was a teaching moment, a few of them answered, "Probably not."
>
> He then took a bucket of sand and began to pour it into the jar until it filled the spaces left between the rocks and the gravel. Once more he asked the question, "Is this jar full?" Beginning to catch on, the class shouted, "No!" Finally, he grabbed a pitcher of water and began to pour it in until the jar was filled to the brim.
>
> Then the teacher asked the class, "What is the point of this illustration?"
>
> One eager student explained, "No matter how full your schedule is, if you try really hard, you can always fit some more things into it!"
>
> "No," the teacher replied, "that is not the point at all. Imagine if you tried to reverse the order, putting the biggest rocks in last. Do you think you'd be able to fit the same amount of material into this container?"[5]

This illustration reminds us of a basic principle of life: if you don't intentionally set the priorities in your life, life's events will prioritize your life for you. Is worshiping God in community with others a "big rock" that gets placed first into the jar of your family life?

PROTECTING YOUR TIME TOGETHER

One of the most important but neglected aspects of relating to others in our digital age is spending actual, face-to-face time together. This is especially true with our family. To grow together, we must spend time together.

With so many demands on our busy schedules and limitless opportunities for leisure, surfing the Internet, and other pursuits, it is necessary to deliberately carve out time to be with our loved ones. This involves setting appropriate boundaries on our work life. Not long ago, I was struck by the story of a father who had promised his son they would go fishing after dinner one night. During dinner, a colleague phoned him with a pressing issue, asking him to come into the office and resolve it. Graciously, but firmly, he declined. "Somebody else can give you input on this, but no one else can be a father to my son tonight." His son was deeply impressed. In saying no to work, his father was saying yes to him.

What families need most is presence. Wives and husbands need to spend time together to grow their marriage. Children need time with their parents. J. J., a friend of our family, is now in his thirties. His father was a man consumed by his work, and as a teenager, J. J. would lie awake in bed, missing him. One evening, he recalls this emotional exchange with his dad:

> Around 11 p.m., I heard the front door swing open and bang into the wall. Heavy footsteps. Then his slow walk. I rose out of bed and approached him.
>
> "Hey Dad, where've you been?"
>
> "I've been working."
>
> "Why are you never home?"
>
> "What? I always come home."
>
> "I don't mean come home. I mean why do you never come home on time? I miss you."
>
> "You have no idea how hard I'm working. Who do you think is putting food on the table? Who do you think is paying for the

cottage? Where do you think our two cars come from? You're an ingrate. What do you want from me? I grew up with nothing. You don't have to work. I have provided you with all you need. What more do you want?"

"I don't want anything. I want you."

We may feel a compulsive need to earn and provide for our loved ones, but often it is more about our need to see ourselves as "successful" than to really provide what our family needs. What our family needs most from us is *us*.

Whether you are a parent, a son, a sister, or a housemate, what people need most from you is *you*. Sometimes loving our family means that we will reevaluate our priorities and overhaul our time commitments. It's easy for us to give lip service to the notion that our families are our priority but still tune them out. Do you answer emails on your phone during family dinner? Are you surfing the Internet while your children play by themselves? It's far harder to say no to these desires than we realize. That's why we need to have an intentional rule that guides us, a commitment that will help us to pursue the things we truly value.

PRACTICING HOSPITALITY

Hospitality is a prized virtue of monastic communities. Benedict's rule says: "All guests who present themselves are to be welcomed as Christ, for he himself will say, 'I was a stranger and you welcomed me.'"[6] Brother Alphonsus served as a doorkeeper in the seventeenth century at a Jesuit college in Majorca, Spain. Each time someone knocked at the door he would reply, "I am coming, Lord!" This practice reminded him to treat each person with as much respect as if it were Jesus himself at the door.[7]

Growing up, my family did not live in a large or luxurious home, but one of our greatest joys was welcoming people who visited and stayed with us. We had a "big open front door," and at breakfast we regularly saw different faces at the dining table. During holidays, extended family members, friends, and people without family in the area would regularly join us. My wife and I now continue this tradition with our family. Thanksgiving and Christmas are not just occasions for our immediate family to celebrate; we invite and welcome others to join us as well.

A good rule of life for family will also include setting a table for Christ as a way of reminding us to welcome friends and even strangers. Thomas W. Ogletree, a Yale professor, writes:

> To offer hospitality to a stranger is to welcome something new, unfamiliar, and unknown into our life-world.... Hospitality designates occasions of potential discovery which can open up our narrow, provincial worlds. Strangers have stories to tell which we have never heard before, stories which can redirect our seeing and stimulate our imaginations. The stories invite us to view the world from a novel perspective ... [and] may enrich, even transform, that world.[8]

PRAYING WITH AND FOR ONE ANOTHER

Another way of knitting one's family closer is by together seeking God in prayer. As we pray together, we grow more aware of God's presence. At Benedictine monasteries, monks gather to pray seven times a day. While that frequency may not be feasible for your family, it is still helpful to create a daily rhythm of prayer. In the morning, take time to express thanks to God for a new day by praying before your breakfast meal. Lay a hand on a child or roommate and bless them as they leave home for school. Express gratitude to God for your health as you take an evening walk or a bike ride. As a household, choose to not just watch the news together but to pray for the suffering of people in another part of the world who have just experienced an earthquake, tsunami, or terrorist attack. At the end of the day, pray with or for members of your family before bed. Through these regular patterns of prayer as a family, you become more aware of the presence of the living God in your midst.

STUDYING TOGETHER

In Western culture, most people study in isolation from others, reading alone in a library or finding a quiet place to think and write. But it is also possible to engage in communal study, learning as a family. Benedictine monasteries typically set aside time each morning for study and communal reading during mealtime.[9] These practices are worlds apart from the typical household in North America where a person watches television around five hours a day.[10] Parents change the culture of *their* household when they make it fun to read, learn, and grow through the Scriptures and other great books that inspire faith in God.

My father grew up in Kagoshima, Japan, in the years right after World War II when most Japanese people were impoverished. Their local bookstore had a policy that parents could buy books for their children and pay later (without interest) when they were able to do so. There was also a secondhand bookstore nearby that sold books for next to nothing. With few other options available to him, as a boy my dad would lie on his futon and read these used books late into the night. While my four siblings and I did not grow up with the same level of poverty, we could not afford many toys. My mom would take us to the neighborhood library each week where we would check out as many books as the limit allowed. My dad promised us, "If there is a book you want to read (that's not in the library), I will buy it for you." Now my siblings and I are all parents of young children. Each evening, in our homes in Vancouver, LA, San Francisco, and Montreal we turn off the TV, sit with our children, and read together.

Julius, a Nigerian man I've become acquainted with, rises each morning with his wife and two daughters to read a chapter of the Scripture together and pray for the day. From the age of five, the daughters have read and taught from the Bible, taking turns leading the family devotions. They've read the entire Bible as a family. This simple practice has bonded them together and created a lifelong resource in their daughters' lives. Rather than glazing over during the Sunday morning sermon, their teenage daughters listen to the preacher's exposition and openly volunteer their opinion on the text during the car ride home from church.

WORKING AND SERVING TOGETHER

Benedict once wrote, "Idleness is the enemy of the soul. Therefore, the community members should have specified times for manual labor."[11] In older agrarian societies, family members worked side by side each day to support themselves. While you may not live on a farm, it is still valuable to find ways to work together as a family. This can be something as simple as doing daily chores or building a tree fort.

As a boy, my friend Jonathan recalls a family tradition called *Family Friday Nights.* "Somehow my parents convinced our entire family [three sons and one daughter] to clean the house on Friday nights. There was a list of tasks for us to complete and we each had our own responsibilities. We usually finished pretty quickly and afterward would get dinner at Mr. Sub and rent a movie. Even though it was cleaning work, I still remember looking forward to those times. The food and movie helped make it fun, but it also felt special to do something together as a family." He adds, "Since my mom cooked, my dad was always responsible for dishes. Without a dishwasher, he would wash and one of us would take a turn drying and putting them away. Eating dinner could go quickly, but doing dishes was a time when we would bond with our dad. He would show interest in our lives and ask questions to learn what was going on. This still happens whenever we visit my parents."

As a ten-year-old boy I talked my way into getting a paper route with the *Vancouver Sun.* I don't remember how many customers I had on my route, but I remember that I bolted my paper rack on my bike's handlebars (ET-style). My BMX was laden with so many papers that it nearly steered itself. I also slung two paper bags over each shoulder like a Wild West gun fighter. I sometimes carried an extra bag on my back Sherpa-style—with the strap of the bag balanced on my forehead.

One year, we had a blizzard. The snow was too deep for me to ride my bike. It was even too deep for us to drive our van. I looked out the window dreading the fact that I would have to *walk* my entire route that day, carrying a heavy load. Sensing how anxious I was, my mom put her hand on my shoulder and said, "Don't worry. In the garage there's a sled. I'll help you pull." At the age of ten, I didn't know much about God, but as we walked along that quiet, snow-blanketed street, I saw the love of God in the footsteps of my mother as she trudged alongside me—"God wearing mittens."

A FAMILY ON MISSION TOGETHER

When I ask parents what their greatest hope is for their children, they often tell me that they just want them to be "happy." Ironically, studies have shown—and spiritual wisdom teaches us—that a person will never be happy if they make personal happiness their goal.[12] Jesus said it is in losing our life in love and service for God and others that we will find it.[13] If we make it our aim to bless others, then paradoxically we find ourselves much happier in the end.

A life of giving and sacrifice is both taught and caught. Patrick is a single father in our faith community with a four-year-old daughter named Claire. He regularly buys food for the homeless near downtown Vancouver and distributes it with his daughter by his side. Their purpose is not just to feed people but to develop a relationship with those they serve. "Claire will wear something fun like antlers or a princess outfit, something that stands out ... and it doubles as a conversation piece. We spend time chatting and not just focusing on giving out the food item. The goal is to develop relationships, an understanding, and grow love in our hearts. Sharing Jesus stems from there but a foundation is laid first." Patrick says, "It's fun and playful. We remember God has a sense of humor too!"

Families do well to develop patterns of serving others in their community. The goal of a Spirit-guided rule is to experience Jesus in every part of our lives and to embody his love *for others*. The ancient rabbis told a story of two brothers who farmed a shared piece of land. One brother was single without any children. The other brother was married with several young children. At the end of the day, the brothers would divide the grain they had harvested exactly in half and each would deposit his grain into his own silo.

One day the single brother thought to himself, "This arrangement of dividing our grain in half at the end of the day is not right. I am a single man with no wife or children to feed. I don't need as much grain as my brother who has a family to support." He thought to himself, "I will give my brother a gift of grain," but then he thought, "If I do that his face will fall in shame. Ah, here is what I will do! In the middle of the night when my brother is fast asleep, I will take some grain from my silo and deposit it into his silo."

Meanwhile, the married brother thought to himself, "This arrangement of dividing our grain in half at the end of the day is not right. I am a married man with many children. They will grow up one day and support me. My brother is single and has no children. When he is old he will have no children to support him. He needs more grain than I do." He thought, "I will give my brother a gift of grain," but then he thought, "If I do that his face will fall in shame. Ah, here is what I will do! In the middle of the night when my brother is fast asleep, I will take some grain from my silo and deposit it into his silo."

And so for nights on end, the brothers passed each other like ships in the dark. One night under the light of the full moon, the brothers saw each other with their sacks of grain and immediately realized what the other was doing. They dropped their sacks and embraced each other because they recognized how great was their love for one another. The rabbis say God turned to the angels and said, "What is happening here makes this a holy place, and I am pleased to dwell here."

Our rule of life is best lived out in our households because those closest to us help refine us so that we become a blessing to God and to everyone around us. A rule that draws the members of our families closer to Jesus and helps us more fully embody his love for others is the greatest gift we can offer God and the world.

QUESTIONS FOR REFLECTION AND DISCUSSION

1. How is a family or household like a furnace?
2. What has been the most challenging part of family life for you? What has been the greatest gift you experienced in a family or a community?
3. What part of the rule (for example: Sabbath, play, time together, study, service, etc.) might be most beneficial for your household right now?
4. What would it look like to pursue that activity together?

WRITING YOUR RULE

Create a record of the blocks of time you currently spend with your family or household in a typical week and then note any adjustments you might want to make based on the information in this chapter. Share this with your family or household members.

PART 4

RESTORE

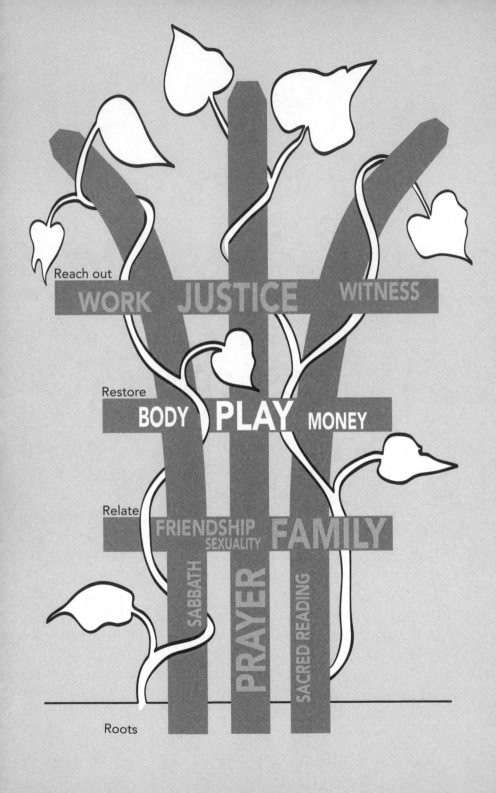

Reach out

WORK   JUSTICE   WITNESS

Restore

BODY   PLAY   MONEY

Relate

FRIENDSHIP   FAMILY
SEXUALITY

SABBATH   PRAYER   SACRED READING

Roots

— CHAPTER 10 —

EAT, SLEEP, SWIM

When I was fifteen, I played football for the North Surrey Lions. When I would look at myself in the mirror I couldn't help but admire how massive I looked ... until I took off my football pads! I was a really skinny kid. Back then I admired my younger sister's naturally broad shoulders. I once told her, "If I had your physique, I could be a linebacker in the NFL." She answered, "If I had your skinny legs, I could be a runway model." Throughout our adolescent years my sister went on countless diets, even going so far as to wear a homemade tracksuit made from Glad garbage bags. I did countless bench presses with my Sears plastic cement-filled weights in our basement. We were both trying in vain to reach our ideal body types, which would forever elude us.

While most of us would like to change a thing or two about our bodies, we tend to view people who are obsessed with working out or dieting to attain a certain body type as vain and superficial. Certainly, excessive exercise, some forms of dieting, and cosmetic surgery can be motivated by vanity. But the care of our bodies through regular exercise, adequate sleep, and healthy eating constitutes a foundational part of our rule, our trellis that supports our life with God. The body, mind, and spirit are interconnected. This means that physical practices are also *spiritual* practices. When we attend to the basic needs of our bodies, we will likely find ourselves more attentive to God and more available to people. Conversely, if we neglect our bodies, we will find that they will eventually scream out for our attention. As Desert Father John Cassian once observed, "If we don't give the body what it needs, it will demand everything."[1]

OUR BODY MATTERS

Historically, Christians have had an inconsistent view of the importance of the physical body. Some Christians, influenced by ancient Greek dualistic thinking, have believed that while the soul is good, the body is evil.[2] The Scriptures, however, affirm that while the body, like the mind and spirit, has been infected by the sin virus and has the capacity for evil, it also reflects the image of God and thus has the potential for good and is worthy of respect and care. In Psalm 139:13–14, David lyrically expresses how marvelously God has crafted each of us: "For you created my inmost being; you knit me together in my mother's womb. I praise you for I am fearfully and wonderfully made." We can easily think this is true of David himself—or at least of Michelangelo's statue of David!—or those who are featured in *People*'s list of the one hundred most beautiful people in the world, but not us with our less-than-perfect bodies. Still, the psalmist affirms that each one of our bodies in all its uniqueness is created by God and is fearfully and wonderfully made.

By becoming a flesh-and-blood human being in the person of Jesus Christ, God demonstrates that he values and honors the human body. If the human body were inherently evil, God never would have clothed himself in one. So God's decision to take on a body—the Christian doctrine of the incarnation—is the highest affirmation of our physical bodies. God blessed our physical bodies, declaring at creation that what he had made was "very good." Moreover, the living God can actually indwell our bodies by his Spirit. According to the apostle Paul, if we belong to Christ, our bodies house the Holy Spirit: "Do you not know that your bodies are temples of the Holy Spirit, who is in you, whom you have received from God? You are not your own; you were bought at a price. Therefore honor God with your bodies."[3] Here we not only see how greatly God honors our bodies, but we also learn that our bodies are not our own—they are on loan to us.

Several years ago when I moved to Southern California to help begin a new church, John and Carol, a couple who traveled up to half the year for their work, invited me to live in their lovely home overlooking the ocean free of charge. I was especially grateful for their generosity, as my salary was only two hundred dollars a month at the time. Because John and Carol had been so generous to me by opening up their house and showing me kindness, I wanted to take good care of their home. When they traveled, I made sure there were no house-wrecking parties. I tried to keep their house clean and in good repair. In a similar way, if we've been given new life in Christ, our bodily "house" is no longer our own but belongs to God — a God who has been breathtakingly generous with us, giving us his only Son so that we can become his sons and daughters. In light of God's mercy to us, we respond by honoring the "house" that God has given to us and entrusted to our care.

THE RESURRECTED BODY

The future resurrection of our bodies (1 Corinthians 6:14) is also a compelling motive for treating them well in the present time. I have a friend who half-jokingly refers to his body as an old Chevy — in need of tune-ups and replacement parts. While our bodies may eventually take on similarities to an old car, they are not destined to disintegrate in a junkyard. The Scripture tells us that our bodies will one day be raised from the dead and we will inhabit glorious resurrected bodies of everlasting splendor.[4] When baseball legend Mickey Mantle was dying of diseases brought on by a life of heavy drinking, he said that he would have taken better care of himself had he only known how long he was going to live.[5] When we understand that we will live eternally and that there will be continuity between our current bodies and our resurrected bodies in the age to come, we have enormous incentive to care for them.

We also see in Scripture that God offers personal and practical care for the body, particularly when we read the story of Elijah.[6] The prophet Elijah, zealous for the honor of God, had challenged the pagan prophets of Baal to a showdown on Mount Carmel. After a stunning victory in which fire rained down from heaven and consumed Elijah's sacrifice, he experienced one of the high moments of his life. Yet soon afterward, Elijah learns that Queen Jezebel, infuriated by his victory over her prophets, has retaliated by threatening to kill him. Physically, emotionally, and spiritually exhausted, Elijah runs for his life—about twenty miles into the wilderness of Judah. Coming upon a broom tree, he collapses and, turning suicidal, prays that he might die. At that moment, an angel touches him and invites him to eat. Elijah looks around, and there by his head is some bread baked over hot coals and a jar of water. He eats and drinks and then lies down again. The angel comes back a second time and touches him and gives him more freshly baked bread and water (1 Kings 19:1–9). When Elijah is depleted, depressed, and physically exhausted, God doesn't offer him a "spiritual" solution. He doesn't give him a passage to read from the Bible, or pray for him, or say, "I know a great therapist." God offers Elijah two long sleeps. Twice, God provides him with freshly baked bread and two long drinks of water. God's care for Elijah is physical, practical care for his body. At last rejuvenated, Elijah runs to Mount Horeb.

We may not be at the same breaking point as Elijah, but each of us needs the gifts Elijah received from God: sleep, food, and exercise. As we receive these physical gifts from God, we will find ourselves in a place where we can flourish spiritually.

THE GIFT OF SLEEP

One of the first things people sacrifice when they are busy is their sleep, hoping that the additional time will help them make headway with their endless tasks. As a younger person, I felt that to be productive, I needed to learn to get by with less and less sleep. I was mesmerized by the example of the Navy Seals, who, as part of "hell week," get by on five hours of sleep. Not five hours a *night*, but five hours for the entire *week*. My experience working in Tokyo in my early twenties reinforced this line of reasoning. As I rode the subway to work each day, I would see that those fortunate enough to get a seat were sleeping. Perpetually overworked and notoriously sleep deprived, Japanese "salary-men" rely upon these subway naps to survive. Some even manage to doze while standing (which is possible when a train is so crowded that you cannot fall over). Like many of my coworkers, I assumed that if I could get by on less sleep, I would be more productive. Thankfully, I came to discover from both Scripture and the hard lessons of experience that getting sufficient sleep is not a liability but a gift from God.

We often think of monks as ascetics who deprive themselves of things that ordinary human beings need. In Benedict's day, monks would actually rise at two in the morning for prayers, but they would also go to sleep at six in the evening so they could enjoy a full eight hours of sleep. In his rule, Benedict encouraged more sleep during the winter months when it became darker earlier in the day.[7] As Benedict realized, if we get enough sleep, we will find ourselves more present to God and more available to others.

If we resist the gift of sleep, we put ourselves at risk. If we are sleep deprived, we are less alert and more irritable. We compromise our immune system and are more vulnerable to all kinds of illnesses. Dr. William Dement, the founder and former director of Stanford University's Sleep Research Center, contends that sleep, more than any other factor (including diet or exercise and heredity), predicts longevity and health.[8] While amounts vary from person to person, he says a typical person needs between seven and eight hours of sleep per night.

It's natural to assume that we know how to sleep—after all, we've been doing it our entire lives. Most people, though, will go through periods where they have some trouble sleeping. Part of establishing a healthy pattern of sleeping may involve relearning *how* to sleep well. Certain practices can be helpful, like disengaging from the computer or other electronic gadgets in the evening. For example, I generally leave my laptop in the office and have chosen not to have a computer at home.

An evening ritual can also help prepare you to sleep. If I have some niggling to-dos that are making me feel restless, I feel lighter if I can offload my mental to-do list onto a piece of paper. If I have trouble falling asleep I find it helpful to recite a Scripture like Psalm 103 or 139 or John 15. I may recollect the day through the practice of the *Examen* that I mentioned in an earlier chapter. This ritual helps me to enter into a prayerful, meditative state as I prepare to sleep. My wife finds it relaxing to read and, especially when we are in Japan, to take a bath before she sleeps. Are there rituals that might be helpful for you as you prepare to sleep?

For some people, napping is a great way to experience refreshment as well. Some may have a job or other responsibilities that prevent them from napping during the day, but others avoid napping because they assume it is a sign of weakness or they feel guilty. Sometimes, when I'm awakened from a nap by a phone call, if the person on the other end asks, "Were you sleeping?" I'm tempted to say, "No, I wasn't" or "I was just closing my eyes," as if sleeping during the day is a shameful sign of weakness. But many people have found napping to be a helpful practice that reenergizes their body, mind, and spirit. The prolific church historian Martin Marty has said that a brief nap increases his energy for hours. For decades he has taken two naps on most days.[9] Winston Churchill, certainly no slouch, understood the restorative value of naps: "You must sleep sometime between lunch and dinner and no halfway measures. Take off your clothes and get into bed. That's what I always do. Don't think you'll be doing less work because you sleep during the day. That's a foolish notion held by people who have no imagination. You will accomplish more. You get two days in one—well at least one and a half, I'm sure. When the war started, I had to sleep during the day because that was the only way I could cope with my responsibilities."[10] Napping is one way to care for our bodies that enables us to be more attentive to God, ourselves, and the people around us.

HEALTHY EATING

When God showed his care for Elijah, he not only provided him with the gift of sleep, he also gave him gifts of freshly baked bread and water. The food Elijah received nourished him, and he was able to run for forty days and forty nights. Like sleep, food is a gift from God. Eating well is a way we can care for our bodies so that we are more available to God and others.

One of the key factors to health and longevity, as we know, is a healthy diet. For centuries, monks have understood how food affects our spiritual lives. The rule of Benedict, for instance, offers clear counsel about eating, requiring monks in good health to abstain from eating the meat of four-legged animals such as beef or lamb but permitting poultry and other two-legged animals, as well as fish and other creatures. The primary reason for the prohibition from eating four-legged animals was the expense: raising or buying four-legged animals for meat required wealth in Benedict's day; by contrast, chickens could forage on the monastery grounds, and wild fish could be caught for free.[11] Saint Benedict wanted to foster prudent spending on food, but he also allowed the monks to spend more on food to promote good health. If a monk was sick and in need of more nutrition or was engaged in strenuous work, then the abbot gave the monks more money to purchase beef and lamb.

Today, a wise rule in regard to food includes prudent spending and an eye for good health. Sometimes, prudent spending and eating healthy food can be in tension with one another. More nutritious food is typically more expensive. Food that is organically grown is good for us and for the earth, but not everyone can afford it. Whenever possible, seek to buy nutritious, organic, locally grown food. One way to resolve the tension between cost and quality is to buy better food, but less of it. A small grocery store in our neighborhood sells only organic, locally grown foods. This past summer, my family and I enjoyed buying delicious, locally produced, homemade ice cream from this shop. The ice cream they sell is a bit more expensive than the commercial brands available in the supermarkets. But we buy the organic ice cream because we prefer to eat better, but less, ice cream. We also buy eggs produced by chickens that are free to roam, chickens without any added growth antibiotics, and beef that is grass-fed. We buy smaller portions of these items because they cost a little more.

It is possible to swing to an extreme position here. Jesus warned us against becoming too preoccupied with what we eat and drink.[12] The wisdom of the Desert Fathers is helpful here as well. They defined gluttony not simply as overeating but also as *being too fastidious in our choices concerning food*. Pope Gregory the Great defined gluttony as not just overeating but as the penchant for eating "costly meats" and having "a need for food to be daintily cooked."[13] In a city like Vancouver, where I live, it's easy for a person to become a "health-food junkie." Clinical psychologists have even coined the term *orthorexic* to describe people who are obsessed with eating health food. They will only eat food they regard as healthy and "pure" and may insist on *only* eating organic food, or *only* fresh foods, or *only* raw food. Their self-identity becomes so wrapped up in their eating choices that, ironically, rather than receiving nourishment from their eating habits, they experience unhealthy amounts of stress. They approach mealtimes with fear rather than joy.

Prudent spending and healthy choices are important, but the Scriptures show us that God created food for our enjoyment as well as our nourishment. God has provided food not merely as fuel for human beings but as a delight to our eyes and taste buds as well. In Genesis 2:9 we read: "The LORD God made all kinds of trees grow out of the ground—trees that were *pleasing* to the eye and *good* for food" (emphasis added). The Bible repeatedly describes the promised land of Canaan as flowing with milk and honey, an abundant place whose fruits were to be enjoyed. Food is a gift that God intended us to delight in. God could have made our taste buds like those of a cow so we only wanted to eat grass—but he gave us the capacity to delight in a variety of flavors and textures, smells and colors. Saint Benedict also directed monks to be generous in their supply of food and to offer a choice of dishes so people could enjoy their meals. Seasonable fruits and vegetables, for example, were to be added to the table. Enjoying good food—which doesn't necessarily mean expensive food—is part of God's gift to us.

In Japan, where part of my family resides, people are conscious about eating healthy foods, but they also believe there that if a person *enjoys* their food it will foster good health. Japanese people believe that being *too* careful, *too* fastidious about food, counting every calorie, cutting out whole categories of pleasurable foods, can backfire—causing unnecessary stress and undermining a person's health. Hediki, a friend from Japan with whom I have enjoyed sailing, is a retired executive who used to work for one of Japan's famous, historic beer companies. He's in his sixties but is full of life and loves new adventures. Like most Japanese men, he enjoys socializing with friends over good food and a beer or two. When his doctor told him that, given his blood pressure, he needed to abstain from drinking any alcohol and to cut out dessert, my friend dutifully complied, only to find his blood pressure actually rise because he was experiencing so much stress and disappointment about not being able to have an occasional beer or dessert!

While we should weigh carefully our doctor's advice and drink in moderation (and there are excellent reasons why some people completely abstain from alcohol), the occasional treat can be *beneficial* for our health, helping release pleasure chemicals like serotonin and endorphins in the brain that promote a sense of well-being. This natural process is part of God's gift to us. The only thing sinful about occasionally eating chocolate or ice cream is that it violates Hollywood's unhealthy, unrealistic commandment around beauty: "Thou shalt pursue a body like what you see on the cover of *Shape* or *Maxim* magazine." It is not a sin to enjoy food. The real sin is to embrace the unrealistic, unattainable standard of beauty perpetuated by the advertising industry.

Eating well nourishes and enlivens us and puts us in a much better position to be fully present to ourselves, others, and God.

FASTING FROM FOOD

Perhaps enjoying food is *not* an issue for you. In fact, you readily indulge your appetite and perhaps even turn to food as a source of comfort—eating not only to satiate your physiological hunger but also to meet an emotional need. If this is true for you, fasting from food[14] may be a practice to consider. Richard Foster says, "More than any other discipline, fasting reveals the things that control us."[15] As is widely known, fasting promotes physical health and healing by resting our digestive organs and detoxifying our bodies. Even more importantly, fasting can help us ensure that God, not food or something else, is the focal point of our lives.

Fasting frees us to feast on God. In our hunger for food we grow to understand our greater dependence on God, and our physical hunger reminds us that we are sustained not bread alone but every word that proceeds from the mouth of God (Matthew 4:4; John 4:32–34). Though Scripture does not command regular fasting, throughout the Bible we see people fasting as a way to express their desire to turn to God in a new way or to hear from him. Fasting also frees up time to pray. When we fast, we realize how much of any given day is consumed by cooking, eating, and cleaning up after meals, and we find we have more space for God.

Fasting, like other spiritual disciplines, should be something we gradually learn to practice. Certain people, including pregnant women, young children, and people with diabetes, should not fast from food. If you are new to fasting, consider starting by skipping a meal or going a day eating simply raw fruit and vegetables and juice and water. Drinking enough water to ensure you are sufficiently hydrated is essential. I typically fast for a twenty-four-hour period once a week. I begin my fast after dinner, and then I skip breakfast and lunch the next day and break the fast with dinner. In the summer I may do a three-day fast. A couple of times in my life, when I have been in special need of discernment, I have fasted for longer periods. If you plan to pursue a fast of five days or longer, you should do further study on fasting and seek the guidance of a physician.

Fasting may sound austere, but you can learn to *love* fasting. During Lent this year, my wife half-jokingly said to me, "You can't fast—you enjoy it too much. If you want to give something up for Lent, give up fasting." Contrary to what people assume, fasting can actually become a genuine delight. If your body is not accustomed to fasting, at first you will feel hunger pangs and experience physical weakness. As you progress in a fast, you will also feel a sticky coating on your tongue—a sign that you are detoxifying. Typically, by the second or third day of your fast your hunger will subside. As you become experienced with fasting, you will feel an energy lift and a heightened sense of God and the world around you. When it comes to care for the body, seek to maintain a wise balance: spend moderately on food, eat healthily, enjoy your food, and fast appropriately. Avoid the extremes of gorging or starving yourself.

THE BENEFITS OF REGULAR EXERCISE

The apostle Paul, writing to his young friend and protégé Timothy, says, "Physical training is of some value, but godliness has value for all things."[16] Paul wants Timothy to see that growth in godliness is immensely valuable. His point is not to downplay the necessity for physical exercise, but simply to put things in their proper perspective. Monks who are part of the Society of St. John the Evangelist recognize the role physical fitness plays in their spiritual lives. Their rule of life includes the words: "So that we can better glorify God in our bodies, each of us shall take responsibility for maintaining his health through regular exercise."[17] Most monks exercise through extensive manual labor as they raise crops, garden, bake, and do maintenance repairs at their monastery.

Whenever the topic of exercise comes up, nearly everyone agrees that it is a good thing *in general*, but most people find it hard to sustain a workout routine for *themselves*. When it comes to building exercise into your rule, the key, as is true of all the elements of a rule of life, is to begin modestly and increase the level of challenge gradually. My younger brother is an artist. I have never heard him describe himself as an athlete. But not long ago, he set an exercise goal: to do one push-up a day. When he got down on all fours, he found himself saying, "Well, now that I'm down here anyway, I might as well do a few push-ups." After a couple months of this routine, he no longer felt challenged, so he downloaded an app onto his iPhone called *100 Push-Ups*. The program asks you to do as many perfect-form push-ups as you can and enter the number into the program. Then *100 Push-Ups* creates a push-up routine for you. Each day it gives you a different number, like ten or seven or twelve. If you are able to do it, it recalibrates your workout so it is just a bit more demanding (if you cannot, it lightens the regimen). The point is not necessarily to do one hundred push-ups but to *gradually* build your stamina. A rule that integrates exercise will likewise enable you to steadily build.

Part of the way we create a sustainable exercise rhythm is to stay with something *long enough* — typically four to six weeks — that it has a chance of becoming an enjoyable habit. When Dr. Bruce Hindmarsh, a professor of spiritual theology at Regent College, was pursuing his doctoral degree in England, the combination of sitting at a study desk for long hours and the perpetual clouds of Oxford sunk him into a fairly serious depression. "I'm not an athlete," he says, "but I began jogging to help me deal with my depression. For the first four weeks it was really hard, but then in weeks five and six, it began to give back to me." Pondering his experience, Bruce remarks, "If we bear the cross, the cross will bear us." If we give ourselves to exercise, after four to six weeks, exercise will start giving back to us. Bruce now says, only partly tongue in cheek, "Running is my Prozac." Stay with exercise long enough for it to become a life-giving habit. If after a couple of months or so you detest your workout, then try a different kind of activity.

Dr. Martin Sanders, a professor of leadership, says that 80 percent of all exercise equipment is purchased in the two weeks before Christmas and the week between Christmas and New Year's. Typically, by the following spring, 85 percent is no longer being used. It sits idly for a year or two and then eventually winds up on Craigslist or eBay. Part of the reason people stop using exercise equipment is because they grow bored of that particular *kind* of exercise. If we enjoy our exercise, we are more likely to stay with it and experience it as a prayerful offering.

I love to run outside, especially in the woods, and when I run I feel a sense of gratitude and joy in God's creation. I also love to swim. Being in water and rhythmically using different parts of my body fills me with a sense of wonder, and I am reminded that I live and move and have my being in God. I don't lift weights these days (other than our wiggling thirty-five-pound toddler), but in the past as I have lifted free weights, I have felt grounded physically and spiritually, as I recall that God is my strength.

For many people, exercising with someone else makes the workout more pleasurable and sustainable. As we might expect, one of the most important factors in determining if a person will stay in shape is whether they have people around them who share their commitment. My ninety-seven-year-old grandmother has only recently "retired" from playing tennis. Some years ago she bragged to me that she was ranked the number-two tennis player in Japan in her age category. I teased her by saying, "Yes, but in *your* age category there are probably only two or three of you still playing." I thought this was a pretty funny thing to say—until she showed me her backhand. Part of the reason she has been able to play tennis so long is because she has played with a set of beloved friends and has enjoyed the social interaction *almost* as much as winning.

Exercise can give us a sense of joy and lead us into a more prayerful space. It clears our minds and our spirits in ways that cause us to be more present to God and others. It also releases the neurochemicals serotonin and dopamine, both of which create a heightened sense of well-being (a phenomenon sometimes casually referred to as the "runner's high"). This common grace may in turn help us to avoid or overcome addictive behavior. Addictions to sex, drugs, or alcohol spring not just from a desire for a novel "high" but also from reduced levels of serotonin and dopamine. When a person senses that something is "missing" because of this neurochemical deficiency, they can resort to desperate measures (and excess) to try to relieve their misery.[18] Rigorous exercise can help to naturally restore the optimal neurochemical levels in our brains that keep us from self-destructive behavior.

As with eating, the goal of exercise is not bodily perfection but availability to God and others. The ideal with exercise is also wise balance—to give each thing in our life its due: no less, no more.

OFFERING OUR WHOLE SELVES TO GOD

Our bodies are not only "fearfully and wonderfully made" but also, if we belong to Jesus, house his Spirit. This means that our bodies are temples of infinite worth. As we have seen, the simple rhythmic acts of sleeping, eating, and exercising enable us to honor the gift of embodied life in a mysterious way, the consequences of which we may not be fully aware of.

People who suddenly become homeless and lose their accustomed routine of bathing and eating three meals a day lose what most of us take for granted, and they experience a sense of disorientation and desolation. Kathleen Norris in *The Quotidian Mysteries* writes about how neglecting the basic acts of self-care—"showering, shampooing hair, washing body, brushing teeth, drinking enough water, taking a daily vitamin, going for a walk"—can signal isolation from reality itself. Norris observes that being willing to care for our bodies is a part of what constitutes basic human sanity, a faith in the everyday. As unremarkable as they seem, these are acts of self-respect, and they honor our maker.[19]

The way we use and treat our bodies, for better or worse, will profoundly shape our spirit and our relationships with God, others, and life itself. Receiving God's gifts of restoration for our bodies is not selfish. In his book *Let Your Life Speak*, Parker Palmer writes, "Self-care is never a selfish act—it is simply good stewardship of the only gift I have, the gift I was put on earth to offer to others."[20] As we receive the gifts of rejuvenating sleep, nourishing food, and invigorating exercise, we in turn are free to offer our *whole* selves as living sacrifices, holy and pleasing to God. There is nothing superficial about this—it is a *spiritual* act of worship.

QUESTIONS FOR REFLECTION AND DISCUSSION

1. How do we know from the Scriptures that our physical bodies are honored by God?
2. What impressed you about God's response to Elijah when he crashed after his showdown with the prophets of Baal on Mount Carmel (1 Kings 19:1–9)?
3. In what way is sleeping a spiritual act?
4. How can we honor our Maker and ourselves through our eating habits? How can we avoid extremes in our eating habits?
5. How can exercise become a joyful act of worship?
6. In what way is care for your body foundational for your entire rule of life?

WRITING YOUR RULE

Draft what a simple, sustainable exercise routine might look like for you. If you'd like, also address any changes you want to make in your eating and sleep habits.

— CHAPTER 11 —

PLAY LIKE A CHILD

A young man wearing jeans and sporting a baseball cap stood in a subway station in Washington, D.C. He crouched down and removed a violin from a small case. Then something very special happened. Most people missed it.

But not everybody.

It was eight in the morning on a Friday in January—the middle of commuter rush hour. For forty-five minutes the violinist played six famous, beautiful pieces of music. During that time, hundreds of people passed by, yet only a few turned to even look at him. In fact, only seven people paused for more than a minute to listen to the music.[1]

One of those who wanted to watch was three-year-old Evan. A cute black kid in a parka, he kept twisting around to watch the violinist while his mother, Sheron Parker, prodded him to leave, eager to be on time for her class. Eventually, she positioned herself directly between Evan and the violinist so that her son couldn't see him anymore. As they left the subway station, Evan tried to pull away to get one last look.

Who was the young man beneath the baseball cap playing the violin? One of the most famous violinists in the world: Joshua Bell. Three days earlier, he had played his violin to a sold-out crowd in Boston's Symphony Hall where people had paid over $100 for a ticket. Now, in the subway station, adults hurried past Bell without even glancing at him. Yet, every single time a *child* walked past, he or she tried to stop and watch.

Adults are so busy, so preoccupied with our agendas and tasks, that we fail to enjoy the beauty right in front of our eyes. Children don't need someone to tell them to enjoy life. They are naturally curious. They find what they like and they do it. But as we grow older, most of us begin to feel the pressure to be "productive." We feel guilty when we take time to enjoy something or stop to play. Most adults don't even know what it means to play.

Play is doing something for its own sake. It might involve entranced absorption—a child can be transfixed at play—and even strenuous effort that leads to joy and gratitude. Play comes in a variety of forms including crafts, painting, acting, dancing, hiking, sports, blowing bubbles, splashing in water, laughing, joking. Whatever its expression, it helps us more fully appreciate how we live, move, and have our being in God.

If we focus our time and energy only on the likes of prayer, study, or social justice, we can become overly intense. Too serious. We lose our joy, our ability to laugh, to delight in the beauty around us. Ronald Rolheiser in *The Holy Longing* says becoming like Jesus is as much about having a relaxed and joyful heart as it is about believing and doing the right thing, as much about proper energy as about proper truth.[2] Gustavo Gutierrez, the father of liberation theology, suggests that having a healthy spirituality involves feeding our souls in three ways: through prayer, practicing justice, and by having good things that we enjoy (friendships, good food and wine, and healthy leisure that keep our souls mellow and grateful).[3] A restorative rule of life, our trellis that supports life with and for God, will certainly include times of play and leisure.

We can become so preoccupied by our endless tasks that we postpone leisure and play to some future time we envision will be less busy. We may reason that when we retire (or when we become wealthy) we will have time to play and enjoy life. I've said to myself, "When things settle down I will resume swimming," or "when our toddler is a bit older we'll take a real vacation." David Steindl-Rast has wisely said that leisure is not the luxury of those who have time, but rather the virtue of those who give to each instance of their lives the time it deserves.[4]

Monks recognize that there is a proper time and place to do certain things: to sleep, eat, pray, work, *and* play. The beauty of living by a rule or rhythm of life is that it gives us a type of "monastic bell" that enables us to give each instance of life the time it deserves (not necessarily the time we feel like giving it). Saint Benedict's rule includes practices and guidelines, but it also cultivates certain *attitudes*. Our attitude toward play will determine whether it becomes part of the contour of our lives. As is true of each part of our rule of life, our attitude here is rooted in God's Word.

GOD INVITES US TO PLAY

We read in the book of Ecclesiastes that God ordains times to play: There is "a time to weep and a time to laugh, a time to mourn and a time to dance."[5] The Lord promised Israel that when he returned to bless Jerusalem, a sign of that blessing would be that the streets would be filled with boys and girls playing.[6] When we play, we mirror our God, a God who plays. We see God in joyful play at the creation of the world. After creating the earth, God steps back and says, "This is very good."[7] God rejoices in his handiwork. We also see in the ancient book of Job how God's creation of the earth inspired him and the angels to express joy. God appears to Job out of the storm and asks: "Where were you when I laid the earth's foundation … while the morning stars sang together and all the angels *shouted* for joy?"[8] What a moment of exuberant celebration that must have been! The oceans and the mountains, the stunning colors of a peacock feather, the beautiful intricacy of a human face, were all designed by a mirthful Maker.

We also see the value of play — of giving expression to joy — in the life of Jesus. Jesus worked hard, but he also took time to savor life. He only had three and a half years to "save" the world, but he chose to spend several of those days celebrating at a wedding in Cana,[9] an event that may have lasted an entire week. When the wine ran out at the reception, Jesus performed his first miracle — creating exquisite wine. He ate, drank, and celebrated with such zest that he was accused of being a glutton and drunkard.[10] Yet he was neither.

He simply enjoyed life and loved being with people. Jesus had an important mission to accomplish, but he took time in the midst of his work to enjoy the company of children and play with them. Some felt that his mingling with children was a frivolous waste of time. Like scrupulous secret service agents, they obstructed the kids' path to him. But Jesus said, "Let them come to me."[11]

Christ continues to "play" through his people and the work of the Holy Spirit. As poet Gerard Manley Hopkins once wrote, "Christ plays in ten thousand places," through our "limbs" and "faces." If Christ indwells us by his Spirit, he plays through us as we play.[12] We not only manifest the Holy Spirit when we "fish" by bearing witness of Christ's reality to a seeking friend but also when we cast our rod over the side of a boat for rainbow trout. We can be a channel of the Holy Spirit as we join the minister in prayer at a wedding ceremony but also when we dance at the reception afterward. Our play is not something separate from our spirituality; it is itself a sign of the presence of God in the world.

GOD'S DELIGHT IN OUR JOYFUL PLAY

Just after our son Joey turned one, we were at a park in our neighborhood where a slim, middle-aged man with salt-and-pepper hair and silver wired-rimmed glasses was lobbing a tennis ball to his dog just a few feet away. Five or six young children gathered around to watch and Joey shuffled to the edge of the group. Each time the dog would jump in the air and catch the ball, Joey would arch his head back and burst into such convulsive laughing that he would wobble, lose balance, and fall on his bum. Seeing Joey's joy, the children in the group began to giggle with glee as well. They pointed to him and chorused, "He likes it . . . he likes it." By then, the dog owner joined in, saying, "That's a happy boy! That's a happy boy!" He took the slobber-covered tennis ball, put it in Joey's hand, and said, "You try it." Joey didn't yet have the motor skills to throw the ball, so I put my hand under his and we did it together. I took immense joy in the contagious joy of my son. Just as we delight in seeing our own children light up with joy, so too does God our heavenly Father.

Some people find this difficult to believe or accept. They may have grown up in homes where the Sabbath was a dreary day of don'ts: *don't* play baseball, *don't* play games, *don't* chew gum. If this was your experience, you may have a distorted image of God, seeing him as someone who frowns at people who have too much pleasure. The truth is that we belong to a God who loves us more than we can even imagine and delights in our joy. He takes pleasure in our pleasure.

WHAT IS PLAY?

But what activities can we consider play? How do we differentiate our play from our work? Very simply, I would suggest that *play is doing something for its own sake.* Though the benefits to play are many (including developing the neural networks in our brain, boosting our immune system, and fostering creativity), real play isn't motivated primarily for some utilitarian result.[13] It's not a business lunch where the real purpose of the meal is something other than the meal (i.e., getting through an agenda). Play is more like a meal shared with a beloved friend. It's something we engage in for its own sake — to enjoy the company of another and to savor the food. In play there is no ulterior agenda. In our recreation we simply delight in the company of God, others, and the rest of creation.

Sometimes we use the word *amateur* to describe mediocrity. With derision we say, "He's such an *amateur.*" We contrast *amateur* with *professional*, someone who performs with "excellence." But the word *amateur* actually means "lover." G. K. Chesterton said, "A man must love a thing very much, if he not only practices it without hope of fame or money, but even practices it without any hope of doing it well." This is the origin of Chesterton's famous twist of the traditional proverb: "If a thing is worth doing, it is worth doing badly."[14] We play when we love something so much that we feel it's worth doing — even if we don't do it particularly well.

My parents, who are now in their seventies, love ballroom dancing. They go a couple of times a week. "We are not good at it," Mom says, "but we love it!" (More accurately, my mother loves dancing;

my dad loves the sandwiches they serve after the dancing is over.) Play is not about being the very best at something. It's about doing it for its *own sake*, for the pure joy of it.

I am not an accomplished sailor, but I *love* to sail. I love being out on the water: feeling the wind in my face; sighting seals, otters, and eagles; eating clams from the beach; relishing the exquisite sunsets. But I have chosen to not race, because I know I am so competitive that if I race, sailing will no longer feel like play, but work, with the goal of winning. As pathetic as it sounds, I know I wouldn't really enjoy the race unless I won.[15] Again, playing is doing something for its own sake. If something becomes *more important* than the play itself, like being the best, or impressing someone, even getting into good shape, it ceases to become play.[16] It is only when we truly begin to get outside our culture's lie that everything is about achievement that we can experience the gift of true play.

PLAY RENEWS US AND HELPS US CONTEMPLATE GOD

Scientists tell us that play renews our minds. Stuart Brown, medical doctor, clinical researcher, and former professor of medicine at the University of California at San Diego, points out that play helps develop the amygdala (where our emotions are processed), the prefrontal cortex (where executive decisions are made), and the cerebellum (which is responsible for attention and language processing).[17] As we know from experience, play also refreshes our bodies. Taking a walk, doing a few jumping jacks, even standing with one foot on a wobble board can energize us. Because mind, body, and spirit are connected, when our minds and bodies experience renewal through play, our spirits are lifted too. Play is sometimes called recreation because it has the capacity to re-create us.

Play can also serve as a window to God. In his autobiography, *Surprised by Joy*, C. S. Lewis describes an experience he had playing as a six-year-old boy. Lewis gazed at a miniature toy garden his older brother had made for him out of moss, adorned with twigs and flowers. As he gazed at that garden, he sensed a voice of joy calling

... arousing in him an "inconsolable longing."[18] That voice of joy, he discovered years later as a professor at Oxford, was the voice of God. Creative times of play opened a path for Lewis—a path that eventually led him to God.

While play can lead us *to* God, it can also lead us *away* from God. Some become so attached to the pleasures of play (which in themselves are gifts from God) that the pleasures become all-consuming—an addiction that controls them. For example, some people enjoy playing video games. There's nothing wrong with that per se, unless the activity becomes an obsession. Recently, the *Washington Post* featured a story about five young men in South Korea who were so addicted to playing video games that they died from blood clots after sitting for several days in the same position.[19] Even if an activity is not inherently sinful, any form of play—tennis, fishing, Pilates, whatever—that causes you to become so obsessed with the activity itself that you drift from God is a sin. We should choose forms of play that draw us to God and others and that connect us most fully to those things which are noble, right, pure, beautiful, and admirable (Philippians 4:8).

Play can lead us to God, and play can help us *contemplate* God. One of the great obstacles to contemplating anything, including God, is our self-absorption. One of the benefits of play is that it lifts us out of our self-absorption. William A. Barry and William J. Connolly, both Jesuit priests, write, "If you have ever been so absorbed in watching a game, reading a book, or listening to music, that you have been surprised at how much time has passed, or how cold or hot you are ... then you know the power of paying attention to something, and you have a personal example of a contemplative attitude."[20] Cultivating a contemplative attitude means learning to pay attention. If you find that you are having difficulty contemplating God, try paying attention to something other than yourself, perhaps nature, music, or art. Begin with anything that helps you fix your attention on something outside yourself.[21]

I personally find the woods to be a powerful place of renewal. There I am drawn outside of myself and am transfixed by the mysterious beauty of God's creation all around me: the different shades of green in the leaves, the rays of sunlight that spill through the branches above me, the cool breeze that runs through the trail—all of these help me to experience the mystery of the Other. My wife finds that art enables her to fixate on something outside herself and enter into a more prayerful attitude. Creation, art, novels, films—even a pet—can free us from our self-absorption and teach us how to contemplate.

So start by doing something you really love: stroll through your favorite park on a sunny day, listen to beautiful music, or spend time with some children who make you laugh. As you do these things, remember God's role in this gift and his generous creativity toward you.[22] By reminding us of the lavish love of God, our play can open a sacred pathway and become a bridge to prayer.

PLAY BONDS US WITH OTHER PEOPLE

In addition to renewing us and deepening our contemplation of God, play also helps to foster deep bonds with other people. When couples feel like they are drifting, a marriage therapist will encourage them to do something fun or new together. As a couple plays together, they often laugh and touch one another. If they are doing something exciting, they will experience a boost in the dopamine levels in their brains, which helps them to bond. As we play with others, we laugh, sweat together, and feel a greater level of attachment to them.

Church boards can notoriously become political and divisive. At our church, board members regularly say to me, "This is one of the healthiest boards I have ever been a part of." While we have our share of vigorous disagreements, one of the reasons we remain relationally unified is because we take time to play with each other. Some of the best times we have had as a board of elders have been hiking, sailing, skiing, and cooking together. These times of play have deepened our relationships, which has made our work more fruitful. A few times each year our church staff will also take time to play together. After our city hosted the Winter Olympics, we decided to go curling together, inspired by the athletes we had seen. Everyone said, "I've never curled before," and it showed, but we had a great time. If people play together, they are more likely to work better together as well.

CREATE A RHYTHM (OR RULE) OF PLAY

Some of you are thinking, "I have no time for play. I don't even have time for things I *have* to get done." And even if I've convinced you of the need to have a rhythm of play in your life, you may feel stymied about rediscovering your "play gene."

Once, when Alfred Hitchcock was directing a suspense film, he and his crew found themselves stuck, unable to move forward with a particular scene. Although they had worked for hours on end, they weren't able to come up with a creative, satisfying resolution. As they sat there, frustrated and discouraged, Hitchcock began telling jokes, one inane joke after another. "What are you doing?" several crew members fumed. "Are you crazy? You're wasting our time!" Hitchcock intuited the problem they were facing—they were trying *too hard* to be creative. "You're pushing," he said. "You're pushing and it won't come by pushing."

You can probably relate. Have you ever had the experience of working on a seemingly intractable problem and then—after taking time to relax, nap, or *play*—experiencing an "aha" moment? Like honoring the Sabbath, we find that play yields its most valuable gifts to us when we think we can least afford to engage in it. Taking time out from your busy schedule, even when it seems unrealistic, may yield benefits that far outweigh the loss of time.

For some of you, play no longer comes naturally to you. You may be wondering *how* to play. If that describes you, try to imagine a friend from your childhood showing up at your door. He says to you, "I have your favorite toy from your childhood in the trunk of my car." Can you guess what toy your long-lost friend has brought? In other words, was there something you loved to do as a child, something that gave you unfettered pleasure? Looking back on your childhood may give you a clue to your "language" of play.

During my childhood and teenage years, I enjoyed playing various team sports: ice hockey, basketball, and football. But as I look back, my favorite memories were those pick-up games of road hockey and football on the cul-de-sac in front of our home. We would play late into the evening, until it was too dark to see the ball. Sometimes, we would argue about whether the ball crossed the goal line, or if hard physical contact was intentional or incidental. I *loved* those pick-up games because I was playing for the sheer joy of playing, not to impress a coach or a girl. While I don't participate in team sports any longer, I still find that physical, informal activities — running, hiking, swimming — are some of the best ways for me to play.

When my wife Sakiko was an elementary school student, she was also a gifted artist. She once entered a multi-province art competition and won second place. For a brief time she considered further art studies, but because she lived in Japan, a country where almost everyone pursues an education to position themselves to get a job, she chose a more practical university major (political science) and then worked as a journalist. Since coming to Canada, however, she has rediscovered her love for art. She occasionally takes a class at a local art college. She does not draw or paint to make money; she pursues art simply for the joy of doing it, for its own sake.

As adults, one of the things that inhibits us from playing is *self-consciousness*: the fear of seeming incompetent or uncool or looking goofy. We may be afraid that if we cut loose and play we will lose credibility and no longer be taken seriously.

I remember the first time our family met my brother's future in-laws. Though there was goodwill on both sides, there was also a certain hesitancy in the air. No one wanted to say or do the wrong thing. Complicating the meeting was the fact that the patriarch of their family was a devout Muslim, while ours was a Christian family in which the eldest son (me) was a pastor. We didn't discuss religion that evening. Instead, we sang karaoke. When my turn came, I was quite anxious. While debating with myself about whether to take a "pass," I stood up from the couch, stepped forward with my left foot, slightly bending my knee and moving the other foot back in a ready-to-fight karate stance. I cocked my left hand on my left hip, and extended my index finger like I was pointing to an eagle on the horizon. Pointing up and then down, I began singing: "Stayin' alive, stayin' alive … ah ah ah, stayin' alive!"

It was a terrible *Saturday Night Fever* imitation, complete with John Travolta's famous disco moves. In spite of myself, I really got into it, but afterward felt sheepish — especially when Mr. Hussein

Pourgal, the Muslim patriarch, muttered something in Persian to his daughter after my performance. I thought I had somehow offended him. Later, I learned that the opposite was true. He had said to his daughter, "I do not know what that man believes. You say he is a pastor. I'm not sure what a pastor is. All I know is he is the right kind of pastor."

We may think that expressing our delight—especially if we look silly—will make us lose our standing with others. But the experience of play, the pure joy of doing something we love, may actually help us build bridges to others.

Above all, keep it simple. Loving play doesn't mean getting caught up in buying expensive, fancy equipment or letting a pursuit dominate our lives. Play is best when it is simple—whether it's the simple joy of taking a walk or throwing a tennis ball to a dog. Let play become a form of prayer for you. Allow yourself to experience God's *pleasure* in your pleasure as you play, whether it is through art, music, sports, or curling up on a couch entering the world of a novel. May your play become prayer as you revel in God's gift of delight.

QUESTIONS FOR REFLECTION AND DISCUSSION

1. As a child, what was your favorite way to play?
2. Why is play an important part of a healthy spirituality?
3. Where do you see evidence that God the Father plays in the Scripture? How do we see Jesus playing in the Gospels? How does the Holy Spirit play through us?
4. Ken described how he felt great delight when his young son played with a dog in the park. Have you ever sensed God's delight in you as you played?
5. What are some of the spiritual gifts that play might offer you?
6. In this chapter we defined play as "something we do for its *own sake*." What is something you enjoy doing for its own sake?

WRITING YOUR RULE

Is there a rhythm of weekly or monthly or seasonal play that you could include in your life? Write this down as part of your rule.

— CHAPTER 12 —

MONEY:
MASTER OR SERVANT?

When I was seven years old my family traveled by ship from London to San Francisco. Our ocean liner stopped briefly on the African coast, sailed through the Caribbean, and on to Florida. While at port, my parents, two of my sisters, and I took a day trip into Miami. Streams of sweat flowed down my legs and my lungs heaved from the effort of breathing the hot, thick air. Under the oppressive sun, my vision blurred and I began to wobble deliriously. We had remembered to bring along some M & Ms, which turned our hands into a smear of rainbow colors, but forgot any water and were tormented with thirst. My parents wisely decided to return to our ship earlier than planned. They waved down a taxi, and I got in the front seat. The driver was a handsome young man with long, wavy blond hair; his shirt was unbuttoned to the middle of his chest—the epitome of cool. Noticing how I looked like a scoop of melting vanilla ice cream about to dissolve into the black asphalt, he must have felt sorry for me. He reached into his pocket and pulled out a fistful of coins. As I cupped my hands under his, he opened his fist and shimmering coins cascaded into my hands. My dad poked the stash with his finger and pointed out a half-dollar coin. He flipped it over and showed me the image of President John Kennedy. I hunched over and clutched my treasure, momentarily forgetting my thirst.

Do you remember the times when you received money as a child? Do you recall the first time you earned a dollar? Perhaps you remember being deprived of money as a child and longing to have enough to buy the things you wanted. As children, we intuitively understand the power of money. It can give us the things we yearn for, the things we desire. Jesus understood the power of money. That may be why he talked about money more than any other social theme. Money is more than just a medium of exchange. As Jesus pointed out, it's a rival god: "No one can serve two masters," he said. "Either you will hate the one, and love the other, or you will be devoted to the one and despise the other. You cannot serve both God and money."[1] More literally, Jesus said, "You cannot serve both God and *mammon*." The word *mammon* comes from the root *aman* which means "something we put our trust in." Like a charismatic lover, money has the power to win our allegiance, the pull to make us lean on it for security, and the capacity to convince us of its promises.

We all know people who have more than enough to meet their needs yet are obsessed with making more. Helen Walton, the wife of Sam Walton, founder of Walmart, said that she pleaded with her husband to ease back on his relentless work. "I kept saying, 'Sam, we're making a good living. Why go out, why expand more? The stores are getting farther and farther away.' After the seventeenth store, though, I realized there wasn't going to be any stopping it."[2] When John D. Rockefeller, Sr., one of the wealthiest people in history, was asked, "How much money does it take to make a person happy?" he gave that immortal answer, "Just a little bit more."

It's not just the rich and the ambitious who fall under money's intoxicating spell. All of us are affected by it … and we all think we would be satisfied with "just a little bit more." Donald Trump was once asked, "How much money would make you feel like you were making enough?" He said, "About 10 percent more than I'm making now." On another side of the world, a man who lives on Smokey Mountain, the garbage dump in Manila, and who supports his family by scouring for pop bottles and recyclable plastic in the rubbish heap each day, was also asked, "How much money would make you happy?" His answer was the same as Mr. Trump's: "About 10 percent more than I'm making now."

How much money do you feel you need to make you happy?

About 10 percent more?

But that 10 percent soon swells to another 10 percent ...

and another

and another ...

Thankfully, when we are united with Christ, our relationship with money is restored to its rightful place in our lives. Martin Luther once said when we are converted to Christ we undergo three conversions: the conversion of our heart, the conversion of our mind, and the conversion of our wallet.[3] In fact, one of the most concrete indicators that a person is genuinely experiencing the converting work of the Holy Spirit is that their relationship toward money is changing.

This change is obvious in the lives of those who take a monastic vow. Those who enter an order and take a vow of poverty move against the current of our culture. They sign away the sum of their worldly possessions to the order or to family or friends outside the monastery. Such a renunciation of worldly goods baffles most of us. We tend to think that monks and nuns are deprived and we pity them. But those who *choose* this way of life don't feel that way. A monk or a nun doesn't simply say no to the pursuit of money and material possessions for the sake of saying no. They say no to money and possessions so that they can say yes to God and have more space in their souls for Christ, for people, and for the things that bring lasting joy. As a result, the decision to renounce worldly goods brings them lasting contentment. They come to realize that they actually need far less than they once imagined.

As a person grows deeper in their union with Christ, they learn that they have a source of wealth that is more fulfilling than money. When a person has more to live *for*, they find they need less to live *on*.[4] The apostle Paul said to his young protégé Timothy, "Godliness with contentment is great gain."[5] Paul was convinced that knowing Christ deeply would lead to greater satisfaction in life. He was convinced of this because he had experienced this mystery in his own life. While in prison he wrote, "For I have learned to be content whatever the circumstances. I know what it is to be in need, and I know what it is to have plenty. I have learned the secret of being content in any and every

situation, whether well fed or hungry, whether living in plenty or in
want. I can do all this through him who gives me strength."[6]

Our culture assumes that in order to be happy we need the power
and security of money. But is this truly the case? Can money buy
happiness? Studies show us that after a person's basic needs are met,
additional money doesn't significantly correlate with a person's happiness. Bill McKibben in his book *Deep Economy* cites research showing that money can buy you a form of happiness—right up to about
$11,000 per capita income (calculated in US currency, 2012 dollars).
After that, the correlation disappears. To be sure, as poor countries
such as India, Mexico, the Philippines, and Brazil have experienced
economic growth, reported levels of happiness have risen. Or consider the "life satisfaction" scores of homeless people in Calcutta.
They were the lowest recorded in this study, but when inhabitants
moved from the streets to a slum apartment, their satisfaction score
almost doubled.[7] Having basic needs met *does* increase a person's
happiness. But once a person passes that $11,000 mark, the data
scatters widely. So even when the Irish were making about a third as
much as Americans, they reported higher levels of satisfaction. Costa
Ricans score higher than the Japanese on happiness, even though
Japanese people have more disposable income than any people on
earth. The "richest" people in the world (according to *Forbes* magazine) are no happier than the plain-living Pennsylvania Amish.[8]

When was the last time you saw a bank advertising a seminar:
"How to Be Content with Less"? To desire fewer things, to live like
money doesn't equal happiness, is truly countercultural. Yet through
a relationship with Jesus Christ, as the Holy Spirit fills us, we discover that there is this narrow path to freedom. We learn to see
ourselves as "rich" in Christ and we begin to value people above our
stuff. And while this transformation of our hearts is a work of sheer
grace—something that God does—grace, as we've seen, works most
effectively in us when we play an active role. What we do with our
money not only *reveals* the priorities of our hearts, but also *deter-
mines* the affections of our hearts.

We know from experience that when we purchase something,
our hearts tend to grow possessive. Buying something often leads

not to the satisfaction of a desire, but to greater desire. Whether we are buying an iPod, a bicycle, a car, or a condo, a part of us remains inwardly focused on this prized possession. There is nothing inherently wrong with buying any of these things, but whenever we buy something we tend to become attached to it at some level. Jesus famously said, "Where your treasure is, there your heart will be also."[9] If we want our hearts to tilt toward God, people, and the things that will last for eternity, we will choose to invest our hearts in those things. A rule of life that helps us wisely steward money will free us to give our *money* to God and to others, so that our *hearts* are given to God, to serving people, and to things eternal.

GRACE GIVING

A good starting point for giving is the tithe: giving a tenth of your income to God. In Malachi 3:10, one of the last verses in the Hebrew Bible and just before the story of Jesus begins, God calls us to trust him with our money:

> "Bring the whole tithe into my storehouse, that there may be food in my house. Test me in this," says the LORD Almighty, "and see if I will not throw open the floodgates of heaven and pour out so much blessing that there will not be room enough to store it."

God makes a clear promise: if we trust him by giving him the first tenth of our income, he will more than provide for our needs. It's difficult for many of us to believe in this kind of divine accounting. Whether we are making a little or a lot, it takes a work of grace for us to trust God with the first tenth of our income. According to the Google Foundation, a typical person needs a base of at least twenty million dollars before they feel they can comfortably give away the equivalent of just a half-tithe (5 percent) out of a place of security.[10] Thankfully, God's grace sets us free from this kind of scarcity thinking and empowers us to give generously without fearing a loss of security.

While the tithe is a good starting place in establishing a rule of life around money, the emphasis of the New Testament is on voluntary giving or what we might call "grace giving." In 2 Corinthians 9:7, the apostle Paul says, "Each of you should give what you have decided in your heart to give, not reluctantly or under compulsion, for God loves a cheerful giver." Giving money is one area where it's especially easy to fall into legalism, so a healthy rule of life will flow from grace. Tithing or giving that is done out of guilt will not energize our relationship with God any more than "loving" a person out of obligation will cause a relationship to flourish. The key is to spend time reflecting on how we've been blessed, how we've been given a treasure beyond measure in Christ. As we do this, our gratitude to God will compel us to give generously.

My wife's family loves animals, and when I was engaged to Sakiko, she was caring for—of all things—a chipmunk. This particular chipmunk had been the runt of the pack and the veterinarian told her that the tiny creature would likely not survive more than a few days. In response, Sakiko named him Forte in the hope that he would grow strong. He not only survived those first few days, but he soon began to thrive. When Sakiko came back to her apartment in the evening after work, Forte would wake up and run excitedly around her apartment doing figure eights. If Sakiko was working on her computer at home, he would scamper up and down the keyboard, pressing on random characters. Sakiko noticed that Forte would take his most treasured possessions—his walnuts—and place them where he slept. I don't know much about chipmunks, but from what I understand this was a form of hibernation instinct for him. Yet what I found most interesting of all was that Forte would take half of his walnuts and put them under Sakiko's pillow. This little chipmunk came to understand that Sakiko was the one who provided for him—she was his family. And out of "gratitude," he wanted to share with her what he had so freely been given.

The point of the story is not to say that we should give God 50 percent of our income. But if we believe God has taken care of us—giving us talent to earn an income, the gift of an education, opportunities to work—then like Forte, as an expression of our gratitude and love, we will want to generously "hide" some of our treasure back with him.

A GRACED LIFE

Grace giving also opens the door to a "graced" life. When we trust God with our giving, we find that God faithfully provides all that we truly need. This has been such a common experience of Christ followers across the centuries that it can begin to sound like a cliché, but the experience of God's provision—whether material or spiritual—always feels fresh when we experience it firsthand. Such was the case when my wife Sakiko was a young adult and a relatively new follower of Jesus.

Her church in Tokyo had decided to purchase a property so that it would have a permanent place to worship. Sakiko felt called to give an offering that amounted to eighteen months of her current salary and set up a separate bank account to save for this goal. She didn't tell anyone what she was doing—only God knew. She had recently left a good-paying editorial job to start a small, not-for-profit publishing company. Her income was meager, and after paying all her necessary living expenses she had very little left to save toward the special offering she wanted to make. She began to accept the idea that she might not be able to achieve her goal.

As the fundraising deadline drew near, something unforeseeable took place. Osaka, where Sakiko's family lives, began bidding for the 2008 Summer Olympics. The city told Sakiko's parents that part of their family's property was required to build a road that would provide easier access to a potential Olympic venue. When the city took their family land, Sakiko's father decided to divide the money he received from the government between his two daughters as a kind of early inheritance. (Remember, he had no idea of Sakiko's giving goal.) Sakiko took her portion of the money and deposited it into the savings account she had opened and the sum totaled her goal: eighteen months of her salary.

Japan is a cash-based society so at the appropriate time she withdrew the equivalent of a year-and-a-half salary in cash. (In my imagination I see her putting the cash in a black briefcase and snapping it shut, then slipping on sunglasses and a dark trench coat to leave the bank.) When she arrived home, she counted out the bills in her bedroom and set it aside. With the cash in front of her, she recognized the magnitude of this sum and felt momentarily conflicted—part of her hesitated to give it away. But the following Sunday, she gave this offering and felt a surge of joy. No one knew the actual amount Sakiko gave except herself, the church's treasurer, and God. The joy lay in the miracle of being able to give this gift.

But then, once again, something unforeseeable happened, something that she wasn't expecting or even hoping for. Over the next couple of months three people (none of whom had any idea what Sakiko had given to her church) felt led to make a donation to Sakiko's small, not-for-profit publishing company. When she totaled the gifts they equaled exactly the offering she had made.

Sakiko felt immensely blessed and loved by God. But her blessing was not primarily material. Because her *company* had received those gifts, she wasn't going to receive a direct personal benefit from them. But as Sakiko gave in faith, God blessed her *spiritually* by showing her that he was aware of her gift and was more than able to provide for all that she needed.

In the Old Testament, God's blessings were often directly tied to the physical land and were most likely to manifest themselves in flourishing crops or an abundance of milk and honey. But in the New Testament era the blessing of God shifted from material to *spiritual* blessings. This means that as pilgrims of Christ, if we give generously to God, he *may* choose to bless us materially, but he may also choose to bless us spiritually instead by giving us a deeper trust in him, a greater sense of contentment, a growing peace while experiencing a painful loss, or a unique opportunity to make a spiritual difference in someone's life.

In biblical times, most people survived on what we would call a subsistence level. Other than kings, aristocrats, and wealthy merchants, people had no discretionary income. For almost everyone, giving would have required both trust and sacrifice.[11] Our society (particularly in the North American context in which I have lived and ministered) is vastly different. Many of us have the potential to make far more income than we actually need to live on. As we make more money, we tend to automatically increase our standard of living. The apostle Paul challenges this tendency by encouraging us to give in a way that is proportionate to our income.[12] Proportionate giving (as the term is used today) simply means we first determine the amount we need (adjusted regularly for inflation) and choose to live on that alone. We then commit to giving the rest away.[13] This approach to finances is rare, but it offers us a beautiful, countercultural way to live.

Although the expression "proportionate giving" wasn't commonly used in the eighteenth century, John Wesley practiced it. As a young man, Wesley calculated that twenty-eight pounds a year would take care of his own needs, so he made a decision to give the rest away. Because prices remained stable, he was able to keep living at that level of expenditure throughout his lifetime. When Wesley first made his decision to live on twenty-eight pounds a year, he was not famous. His income was about thirty-eight pounds a year. In later years, income from the sale of his best-selling books would earn him about 1,400 pounds a year, yet he continued to live on the same amount—twenty-eight pounds—and gave the rest away.[14]

Sarah, a member of our faith community, told me that when she was twenty years old, living as a college student, she loved drinking wine, frequently partied, and boldly extolled the virtues of Nietzsche's philosophy. Yet secretly she was afraid of wasting her life and leading a meaningless, mediocre existence. She decided to go on a mission trip to a very poor part of Nepal with the Christian nonprofit organization Operation Mobilization (OM). It was an experience that changed her life, completely altering her relationship with money and possessions. "I was absolutely blown away by the generosity of Nepalese people," she said. "They were destitute. They had no money, but they gave so sacrificially to each other, and when they had me over for dinner they prepared their very best." At the end of the summer, Sarah met with the leaders of the mission. She had been so deeply moved by the "unbridled kindness and hospitality of the poor" in Nepal that she asked her leaders, "How can I express my gratitude to God? I want this summer to be more than a fleeting experience, more than just another page in the photo album of a tourist." One of her mission leaders replied, "Why don't you make a commitment to express your gratitude to God [over your lifetime] through proportionate giving?"

In other words, "Why don't you assess what you'll need to live on, and then plan to give the rest away?"

Up to that point in her life Sarah had been giving 10 percent of her income but nothing more. Even *that* tithe felt painful to her at the time. Ziggy, a college friend who would later become her husband, encouraged her: "If our financial giving ever stops being painful, then we aren't giving enough." Although Sarah was just an undergraduate student at the time, she made the commitment. "Some years are more financially comfortable than others, but we find we can always afford what we truly require.... Every year, regardless of our combined income, we've made an effort to increase our giving and to ensure it's always a little painful. Our goal is to give away 80 percent. We're not there yet, but last year we upped our giving by 5 percent more."

Like Sarah and Ziggy, when we recognize how generous God has been to us, we want to express our gratitude by becoming radically generous. God calls us to give the first fruits of our income to him, but we should never forget that *all* of our money belongs to him. But this leads to another question: How do we decide what to do with the remaining 93 or 75 (or whatever) percent of the money that we don't give away? How can we be good stewards of the money that we spend, save, and invest?

EXAMEN-ING OUR FINANCES

One approach to carefully thinking through this issue of financial stewardship would be to apply the practice of Saint Ignatius's *Examen* (a daily review). As we consider our discretionary spending, saving, borrowing, or investing, we can ask ourselves, "Where am I experiencing feelings of joy and peace? Where am I connected with God (consolation)?" We can also ask, "Where am I experiencing sadness, apathy, and a sense of disconnection from God (desolation)?" Ignatius would counsel us to choose to invest our money in the things that lead us to experience greater joy and peace in God.

Even *initial* happiness is no sure proof of wise spending if, over time, we find ourselves drifting from God. We do well to examine the entire experience — beginning, middle, and end — and watch for the "tail of the snake" (a symbol of Satan). While we may initially experience joy in a purchase, in the end the things we buy can lead us to feel even more distant and disconnected from God. For example, some people may find momentary pleasure in shopping. Yet the joy of shopping, much like a drug, fails to bring lasting happiness. It may even leave us feeling emptier than before.

Not all shopping, of course, leads to this sense of desolation. Seeking to find just the right gift for a family member or a friend can be a joyful experience. Some people find shopping an enjoyable way to spend time with a friend as they exchange advice about the merits (or demerits) of a purchase and catch up on their lives. Obviously because we live in a market economy there are many things we simply need to buy for our life and survival in this world. And yet we should take time out to pray for guidance, thinking through how a discretionary purchase connects us to or isolates us from God. This type of prayerful, thoughtful examination of potential purchases also tends to decrease our impulse buying and the remorse that can accompany it. Praying before a purchase provides time to reflect and to discern whether our desire for this object or investment is something that honors God.[15]

Prayerful reflection about buying a larger home might lead us to conclude that our desire springs from wanting to impress our parents or to keep up with friends or coworkers. On the other hand, prayerful reflection may lead us to conclude that because we have a growing family, we genuinely need more space. Our rule enables us to experience *every* part of our lives as sacred. Praying before making significant purchases allows us to use our "worldly wealth" to draw close to Christ.

SIMPLIFYING OUR LIVES

As friendship with Christ changes our hearts and our desires we may find that some of our material possessions not only fail to bring us true fulfillment, they actually come between us and God. We may experience a desire to de-clutter our lives so that we spend less time and energy cleaning, maintaining, protecting, and worrying about our stuff. As we offload our possessions, we may feel lighter, but we may also discover that not everyone is as enthusiastic as we are about our choice to simplify. Choosing the way of simplicity may prompt some to wonder if we've lost our minds. When monks enter a monastery and take a vow of poverty, giving away their worldly possessions, some people think that they have gone crazy. Others feel sorry for them.

But monks don't choose the way of simplicity because they are crazy. James Martin, a Jesuit priest, graduated from the prestigious Wharton School of Business and worked in finance for General Electric for several years. He describes entering into the Jesuit community as a novice and the experience of giving away his possessions:

> My money and car went to my parents. My suits would sit in my parents' house in case the novitiate didn't work out. (I wasn't taking any chances.) The rest of my clothes went to Goodwill Industries, which would distribute them to the poor. My books went to friends who dropped by one sultry afternoon to scour my bookshelves. "I wish more of my friends joined religious orders," said one friend.... [Writing more than 20 years later] I can still remember the initial burst of happiness I felt. How liberating it was! No more worrying about whether my suits were the proper shade of gray, my shoes the right brand, my ties the appropriate hue, no more worrying about whether I should rent an apartment or buy one. No more worrying about whether I needed a new this or a new that.[16]

While you may not take a formal vow of poverty like James Martin, you can also feel the joy that comes from simplifying. Resist the cupid arrows of the advertising industry by muting advertisements on television and choosing to *not* buy the latest gadget just because everyone else seems to have one. Learn to distinguish between wants and genuine needs and you will enjoy more of the inner freedom that springs from simplicity.

Perhaps you may even feel led to take a further step by giving away something that you truly value.

THE JOY OF GENEROSITY

As a boy of five or six living in London, I remember playing at the home of a friend who lived down the street. I was enamored by his toy-doll version of a Buckingham Palace mounted guard with a gleaming silver helmet. A long plume of white horse hair hung down from the top of the helmet, and he was clothed in a ceremonial red tunic, covered in part by his shiny, metal chest armor, his white riding pants, and tall black, imitation leather boots. As I said, I was enamored.

In fact, I was so taken by this figure that when my friend offered to give it to me as a gift, I was speechless, incredulous — as I well should have been. As I was getting ready to leave, my friend's mother approached me at the door and said to her son, "Ken really doesn't want *that* toy — he really wants *this* doll," and she handed me a worn-out G.I. Joe figure dressed in green army fatigues and missing an arm. "He lost his arm in war — he's a real hero," she reasoned.

Again, I was speechless. Even as a young boy — although saddened by my reversal of fortune — I understood the economic dynamics of the situation and why this mother wanted her son to keep the desirable, new toy and have him give away the old, broken doll that he no longer played with. Today, as the parent of a toddler, I can't anticipate exactly how I would respond if my son were five and wanted to give away his most valuable toy, but I hope I would seek to encourage him to go for it because there is something beautiful and God-like in giving away something that is precious to us.

Unfortunately, as we grow older, our tendency to spontaneously and naturally give away our valuable possessions often grows cold. Some time ago, I went bike riding with a friend here in Vancouver. His family has season tickets for our local hockey team, the Canucks, and we were riding on a day when the Canucks were playing in a historic game seven of the Stanley Cup Finals. (The cultural equivalent in the United States would be your home team playing in the Super Bowl hosted in your city.) I asked him, "Are you going to the game tonight?" "No — I decided to give my tickets away [tickets worth thousands of dollars]." Knowing that he was a big hockey fan, I asked him, "Are you *okay* with that?" I imagined there would be a tinge of regret in his response, but instead he simply said, "I wanted to *show* kindness to this person ... and so I was glad to give away the tickets." He beamed with joy.

Worldly wealth comes to us as we accumulate things. But in the end, the things we accumulate fade, decay, and return to dust. But there is an otherworldly wealth that comes from the freedom we gain when we give things away. John Chrysostom, an eloquent Church Father, observed that in a theatrical play things are not always as they seem: sometimes a poor man will play the role of a wealthy character and a truly wealthy person might act in the role of a poor man. In a play like this, those who *seem* rich may really be poor and those who *seem* poor may in fact be rich. So it is in life. Sometimes those who seem wealthy are really poor. And sometimes those who seem poor are truly rich.[17] Those who are free to give away what they have are truly wealthy.

We began our chapter by reflecting on the power of money to enslave us, but money, if given freely and used wisely, also has the power to draw us to God and to serve others in love. Money doesn't have to be an idol in our lives. It can serve as a tool that helps us to love God deeply, love our neighbors tangibly, and cultivate our palate for things eternal.

QUESTIONS FOR REFLECTION AND DISCUSSION

1. What was your first memory of money as a child?
2. Do you agree one of the most concrete indicators a person is genuinely experiencing the converting work of the Holy Spirit is that their relationship toward money is changing? Has this been true for you?
3. Recall the story of Sakiko's chipmunk Forte. How does "grace giving" enable us to express our trust and gratitude toward God?
4. Have you ever experienced a special material provision from God? What was your response?
5. Do you feel called to simplify your life in some way? In what way would this be difficult for you? What would be the gift in that?
6. Describe a time when you have experienced joy in giving something away. What might help you grow in generosity?

WRITING YOUR RULE

Describe what joyful "grace giving" might look like for you.

PART 5

REACH OUT

— CHAPTER 13 —

THANK GOD IT'S MONDAY

During the 1960 Democratic primary, a young senator named John Kennedy was campaigning in rural West Virginia. As he was standing by a coal mine shaking hands with the miners, one of them came up to him and asked, "Is it true that you're the son of one of the richest people in the country?" Kennedy, surprised by the question, said, "I guess so." At this, the man scowled, "Is it true that you've never really done a day's work with your hands?" Kennedy nodded his head. The miner then exclaimed, "Well, let me tell you this ... you haven't missed a thing!"

Most people believe that work, particularly work that involves difficult manual labor, is a necessary evil—something they would avoid if they could. Even those who hold "white collar" jobs often feel this way about their work.

I recently had coffee with a friend who shared that when he was a university student he made it his goal to work as a stockbroker so he could retire by age forty. Now, having worked as a stockbroker and nearing his fortieth birthday, he sighed, "With the downturn [in the markets] I likely won't be able to retire until I'm forty-five ... I don't like my work. I'm looking forward to life beyond [it]."

Today, you'll hear people talk about "Freedom 45 or 55," meaning that they hope to be able to retire at forty-five or fifty-five and be free from their job. Others harbor simpler dreams. "I live for the weekend," they say. "*That's* when my real life happens, when I'm doing something other than my work."

Such a perspective is hardly unique. Throughout history people have viewed work as something unpleasant that has to be done. In the Babylonian creation myth, the *Enuma Elish*, a battle breaks out among the gods. Marduk emerges as victor and creates a world from the body of his arch enemy Tiamat. The other gods say, "Now that you have created the earth, you have to work to keep it up!" To which Marduk responds by saying: "I will create a lowly creature called 'man' to take care of it." In this account of our origins, the gods scorn work and create human beings to do the manual labor they don't want to do. Many intellectuals hold a similar position. Plato and Aristotle, for example, viewed work (especially physical work) as debase—something which degrades our minds and bodies.

Must our work be seen as a prison sentence, a result of the curse, something where we "do our time" and from which we seek an early escape? If so, what a tragic conclusion for the vast majority of us who will spend most of our waking hours working!

GOD THE WORKER

The Scriptures look at work in an entirely different way. Unlike the *Enuma Elish* or the Greek philosophers, the biblical account of work shows us that God works and gives us meaningful work to do that serves an important purpose. In Genesis 2:15 we read: "The LORD God took the man and put him in the Garden of Eden to work it and take care of it." *Before* Adam and Eve turned away from God in the Garden of Eden and sinned, *before* the curse came into our world, they were working. Thus work was not the result of the fall and the curse of sin but is a natural part of who we are, something we were created to do. Even in the glorious life to come, Jesus hints there will be new kinds of work for us to undertake (Luke 19:11–27).

When I served as a pastor in California, one of my parishioners spontaneously dropped in on me at home while I was working in the garden. When she saw me down on my knees pulling weeds, she blurted out, "It's good to see you finally doing some *real* work!"

The truth is that we mirror God when we work, and in the very first pages of Genesis we see God working in ways that we would characterize as both "blue collar" and "white collar." On the blue-collar side, God gets his hands dirty when he creates human beings. He blows into man's nostrils the very breath of life. The name of the first man, *Adam*, literally means "from the earth." In the opening pages of Scripture we also see God employed as a gardener, planting trees and crops.[1] But God is also engaged in white-collar labor. A moment before he gets his hands dirty in making man, we see God employed as an architect designing the universe. His spoken word creates the world, the plants, and the animals, arranging and ordering them according to his purposes.

We don't know much about Jesus' life between ages twelve and thirty, but he likely spent most of this time working. According to the gospel of Luke, Jesus followed his foster father into his trade as a *tekton*, which is usually translated "carpenter."[2] As a carpenter, Jesus would have been involved with selecting the right kind of wood, negotiating a fair price with his vendors, and helping build or renovate homes in his neighborhood. As James Martin points out, *tekton* may have also been used to refer to what we would today call "a day laborer."[3] This means Jesus may have done other kinds of manual labor: working on construction sites, hoeing fields, and harvesting crops. Given Jesus' range of work experience, it's not surprising that many of his parables used workplace imagery: building a house, sowing seed, pruning vines. During Jesus' final three years on earth, his work shifted to teaching and mentoring. Jesus said, "My Father is always at his work to this very day, and I too am working."[4] In the book of John we also see the Spirit at work: teaching us, convicting us, and guiding us.[5] If we are indwelt by the Holy Spirit, he works through us not only when we share the gospel but when we make a sales presentation at work, not only as we build a school as part of a mission trip in the Dominican Republic but as we build a house as a day laborer. God's continual engagement in manual and mental work reveals that work is intrinsically good.

CO-CREATORS WITH GOD

When we work, we co-create with God. God placed Adam in the Garden of Eden not to contemplate it or lounge in it but to *work* it.[6] As Genesis 2:5 notes, "no shrub had yet appeared on the earth and no plant had yet sprung up, for the LORD God had not sent rain on the earth and there was *no one to work the ground"* (emphasis added).

Though there is nothing that God cannot do on his own, he has chosen to co-create with us. The apostle Paul says, "I planted the seed, Apollos watered it, but God has been making it grow."[7] We may plant a seed. Someone else may water that seed. But God causes it to grow. God's work is done in *partnership* with us. British author and preacher John Stott told the story about a Cockney gardener who showed a pastor the beauty of the garden he tended—its flowers were in full bloom and its borders perfectly trimmed. Deeply impressed, the pastor spontaneously cried out, "Praise God from whom all blessings flow!" The gardener was unhappy, however, that God should get *all* the credit. He retorted: "You should have seen this garden when God had it all to himself!" The gardener was right. Without a human gardener, that garden would not have been what it was.

Your work may not *feel* particularly spiritual, but if it is legitimate work, you are co-creating with God. Leighton, a young man in our faith community, arrived in Canada from Australia a year ago. At first unable to find work in his professional field, he signed on with a temp agency. One of his first jobs involved shoveling heavy gravel that had been mixed with clay at a site where townhouses were being built. It poured rain all day. At the end of the day, though his hands were blistered and his back sore, Leighton was beaming as he rode the bus home because his foreman had praised his work and asked him to return the next day. He ended up working on the site for nearly a month, serving as the "extra hands" to do the "heavy lifting," or the dirty work others on the crew didn't want to do. Reflecting on the experience, Leighton shared: "I remember stopping for a moment to look around and think—wow—how incredible to take a pile of timber, siding, shingles, and pipes and turn them into a house. I was helping to create a safe haven for a family. In my hammering and shoveling I had an opportunity to mirror the work of my Father in heaven in the world that we live in today."

Even while engaged in the grueling, menial labor of building a house, Leighton sensed he was an instrument of God, co-creating something good for others with his Father in heaven. When we feel the satisfaction of making something—whether with our hands or with our head—alongside the Creator, our work will not seem like a prison sentence. We will experience it as a fulfilling part of our rhythm of life.

Our work can even become part of our trellis where we grow our relationship with God. Dallas Willard contends that the *primary* place of our spiritual formation is not in our church or small groups or fifteen minutes of reading the Bible and praying, but our workplace or school or at home as we change light bulbs or diapers. "To not find your job to be the primary place of discipleship is to automatically exclude a major part, if not the most, of your waking hours from life with him. The gospel turns your work into a spiritual formation training center."[8]

The ancient monastics certainly viewed work as the primary place to grow toward union with God. They saw it as foundational to their training in godliness. In Benedict's sixth-century world, nobles were never expected to work a day in their lives and people routinely employed slaves to do the menial work of manual labor. In this sense, monasteries were revolutionary communities. In the monastery, you would see everyone—those of noble birth and those of common birth—working in the kitchen or in the fields. Work was not seen as a curse but as a gift; work was a way to unite with God and serve the larger community.

PRAYER SANCTIFIES OUR WORK

You may not live in an agrarian monastic community, but your work can still be an essential part of your rule of life, a portal to God and a way to reach out to others. For the monastics, work was sanctified by prayer. Saint Benedict's rule encouraged rhythms of work with the hands and the head interspersed with times for prayer (the divine offices) and rest, so that all of life *including* work was devoted to God.[9] For monastics, this blending of work and prayer drew inspiration from the apostle Paul's admonition that believers should *literally* pray without ceasing.[10] Benedict's predecessor, John Cassian, encouraged the brothers under his care to engage in simple manual labor such as harvesting crops or weaving baskets so that it was possible to abide in *constant* prayer while they were working. As you can imagine, this proved to be exhausting for most of the monks. Even Cassian appeared to question his own prescription in his later writings, where he admitted that this "method of unceasing prayer proved harder to practice than expected."[11]

In contrast to John Cassian, Benedict had a somewhat different attitude toward work. As we noted earlier, many have summarized Benedict's approach to work with the famous dictum, *laborare est orare*— "to work is to pray." For Benedict, work *in itself* has value as a devotional act toward God. To be pleasing to God, work does not require *literal* unceasing prayers or other "spiritual" activities offered alongside it. Simple work done for the purpose of glorifying God was prayer in and of itself. Conversely, prayer was also considered work and was called *opus Dei*, or the work of God. Benedictine monks did not draw a sharp line between their religious engagements and their common, worldly labors.[12] Their rhythms of prayer and work enabled them to experience their manual labor or their study as prayer. And when prayer is a regular rhythm of our lives we too can experience our work as prayer. Many of us are already in the habit of praying before our meals, but why limit our prayers to this time? We can pray before we write, paint, perform surgery, balance the ledger, pour concrete, prepare a meal, or pull weeds. In this way, we are consciously seeking to set apart our work for God and his purposes.

Some years ago, my friend Alvin Ung left his work as an executive for an investment company in Malaysia to study theology in Vancouver. "While at graduate school," Alvin said, "I read about ancient Christians who inspired me to pray without ceasing. It sounded impossible, but I tried to put it into practice as I wrote theological papers. I prayed before my assignments. Writing prayerfully, without anxiety or rush, I would thank God for the insights. Each keystroke would be an act of worship. When the work was done, I thanked God for helping me. Slowly I began to see that my work—and the process of working—could be a form of prayer." When Alvin first returned to the marketplace he felt stressed out and too busy to pray:

> [Then] I was struck by a simple thought. I should regard my work-place as a "monastery" where God is already present. I could pray quick short prayers for my colleagues during work. During lunch, I imagined Jesus Christ as our unseen conversation partner. When I felt stuck, I would ask God for help. So there were lots of oppor-tunities to pray, because I felt stuck so many times a day! Slowly, I began to realize that God had been keeping company with me all this while ... even when I did not naturally turn to God.[13]

While visiting the Musée d'Orsay in Paris, my wife and I were beautifully reminded of this reality that all of our work is done in God's presence when we saw *The Angelus* by Jean-François Millet.[14]

The painting depicts two peasants taking a moment during their work in the fields to bow their heads and pray as the setting sun gently bathes the land. On the horizon behind them is a church steeple, whose angelus bell (hence the title) is calling people to prayer. Yet if you look carefully at the sun's rays, you will notice that they do not fall on the steeple, as you might expect, nor even primarily on the couple as they stand praying, but on the wheelbarrow, the pitchfork, and the basket in which crops have been gathered at the couple's feet. By casting light on these objects, Millet intimates that God is present not only in our church life and in our formal prayers but in our everyday working life as well. Whether we work with hands or our head, whether we are paid or a volunteer, our work is *coram deo*—done before the face of God. Like the Benedictines and this peasant couple, as we take time to weave brief prayers into our day we are reminded of the value of our work. As we pray we become conscious that our work *itself* is an offering to God, an act of worship. This awareness in turn will influence the quality of our work.

As I noted in earlier chapters, when I completed my undergraduate degree, I began working fourteen-hour days at the Sony Corporation in Tokyo. Although I was making far more money than I had ever made before, I felt like I was losing my soul. To counter this trend, out of sheer desperation more than anything else, I put a few boundaries and simple practices in place in my first attempt at a rule of life. I stopped working weekends and renewed the practice of keeping Sabbath. I got involved in a small church about a ten-minute walk from my apartment. During my morning commute, although nodding off and half asleep, I would spend some time praying and offering my workday to God.

This simple rhythm of praying in the morning to offer my day to God slowly changed the way I worked. Over time, I began to focus less on the money I was making and my professional advancement and came to see that I was doing my work not just for a company but for God.

You might think that this would make me less driven at my job, that I'd work more hours "for the Lord" and less for the company, investing more into my pursuits outside of work. And while it's true that I was spending less time at the company, I found I was actually doing higher-quality work when I was there. Echoing the words of the apostle Paul, I found that I was able to "work at it with all [my] heart, as working for the Lord, not for human masters."[15]

A couple of years later I transitioned to Boston to attend seminary. Before I left my job, my manager complimented me by telling me that I would always have a job at Sony if I wanted it. Though he wasn't a Christian, he saw that my commitment to work for the Lord was good for the company. My awareness of God's presence also made my work feel more meaningful.

Much of life consists of obscure, mundane work: washing dishes, writing memos, filing reports, grocery shopping, vacuuming. As we develop the practice of directing our attention to God, even the most menial tasks can become prayerful. For Brother Lawrence, "common business," no matter how trivial the task, was still a rich occasion to be in the presence of God. "Nor is it needful that we should have great things to do," he affirmed. "We can do little things for God; I turn the cake that is frying on the pan for love of him, and that done, if there is nothing else to call me, I prostrate myself in worship before him, who has given me grace to work; afterwards I rise happier than a king. It is enough for me to pick up but a straw from the ground for the love of God." With God, Brother Lawrence cooked meals, scrubbed pots, and ran errands. And so can we. The more conscious we become of being with God in our work, the better we are able to prayerfully improve the quality of the work we do.[16]

PRAYER HELPS US DISCERN

For many people today, even those who have set office hours, there is no longer such a thing as a strict "nine-to-five" job. Our laptops, smartphones, and iPads contribute to a feeling that we must always be "on" and available. We hunch over our laptops, stare at our phones, and tune out the world with our ear buds. Is it any wonder that we find it increasingly hard to pay attention to God and to the subtle shifts inside us? We lack times of prayerful silence and solitude in our lives, and this makes it difficult for us to hear the "gentle whisper" of the Lord (1 Kings 9:12).

A man I know named Charlie faced a moral dilemma at work. As the chief financial officer of a major fast-food company, he was asked by the company chairperson to exaggerate the potential future earnings of the business in order to inflate the stock price. Thus, when the company was sold to another corporation, the executives would reap a financial windfall. Charlie had recently entered into a relationship with Jesus Christ and he felt conflicted, not knowing what to do. He certainly didn't want to be dishonest and intentionally mislead people. On the other hand, as the sole breadwinner for his family, he didn't want to lose his job either. Charlie was flown to New York City to make a presentation before a group of investment bankers. In the hotel room the night before, he found that he couldn't sleep. Instead of working on his laptop or channel surfing, he stayed up all night praying to his "new friend" for guidance. That night, his hotel room became a monastery, and though Charlie didn't receive an oracle from God, he felt a deep peace as he spent time with him.

The following morning, just before he was scheduled to make his presentation, he ran into the chairperson in the hallway. The chairperson urged him to make the dishonest presentation with the glowing numbers. But Charlie knew that he couldn't do it. He said to the chairperson: "I can make a presentation about our future with great enthusiasm, but I cannot lie about the numbers."

In response, the chairperson gave him an ultimatum: "Make the presentation or get off the team."

Moments later, Charlie found himself calling his wife to let her know that he had just been fired. "Great, come on home," she replied. Charlie was convinced that Jesus had led him to make the right decision by refusing to lie, even though his decision had cost him his job. Later, as he sat with his wife at dinner in their home, Charlie told her that this was the best business decision he had ever made. Glancing down at the fish on his plate he told her, "There has never been a day when God has not provided all that we need."

Charlie was new to faith, but spending time with Jesus and making room for the Holy Spirit to speak to him gave him the wisdom he needed to discern God's will and the courage to live it out. Unlike monks, we cannot retreat to the desert or cave for an extended period of time. Yet we can still find ways to unplug in a hotel room, an office, or a car, creating contemplative places where we can attend to the guidance of the Holy Spirit. As we set aside time to learn about God's character through the Scriptures, we come to know what God likes and dislikes. We become people who intuitively discern what pleases or displeases God. Our prayers may lead to clear direction from God. But even when we don't have absolute clarity on a decision we will find that spending time with God helps us better understand his preferences and passions. This enables us to develop a discerning heart that will guide us to honor him in our work.

Don owned a series of car dealerships. Through a self-study of his business, he discovered that men were getting better deals on vehicles than women, and that Caucasian males were receiving the best purchase price on cars while black women were getting the worst prices. In essence, he saw that the black women, many of whom were living on lower incomes, were basically subsidizing the car purchases of the relatively wealthy Caucasian males. By paying more than the market value for their cars, these minority women were enabling others to get away with paying less than the market value. As a business leader who follows Jesus, Don felt that this was not just. Appealing to his employees, he suggested that they put an end to this discrimination against their customers by fixing a fair "price is price" sales policy on cars. Don said to them, "As a Christian, I believe we have to be willing to sacrifice some of our financial profits [to serve justice]." His employees, even those who were not religious, agreed with him.

However, after Don adopted this new fixed-price policy, the profits at his dealerships dropped by about 10 percent. Many Caucasian males decided to shop for cars elsewhere, looking for the best price they could find. His employees noticed the downturn in profits and wondered whether they should go back to the old way of doing business. In the end, however, Don and his employees agreed that rather than reverting to the old, discriminatory sales techniques, they would work to become more efficient and effective by implementing better business practices. By doing this, they were able to cut their profit loss to only 5 percent (there is no guarantee that just because you do the right thing before God and work hard that your profits will grow). Even though the business was less profitable, Don's employees made it clear to him that they were proud to be part of a company that was committed to doing the right thing. Those who seek God understand that part of the purpose of a business is to achieve a fair return on their investment. But the bottom line can never be the bottom line. Businesses should also seek to avoid activities that oppress the poor and vulnerable, taking advantage of others for financial gain, activities that are opposed to the character and heart of God.[17]

PRAYER AND STABILITY

Prayerful discernment can also help us know whether to stay or leave a particular workplace. Work that was once invigorating and fulfilling can become frustrating and painful, and our first impulse is often to leave our job. While there may be times when God gives us the freedom to leave, there are also times when God may call us to stay in a challenging, difficult situation. While praying in the Garden of Gethsemane, seeking to avoid the humiliation and pain of the cross, Jesus pleaded with his Father, "If you are willing, take this cup from me; yet not my will, but yours be done."[18] Yet God called him to stay on the path of the cross so our sins could be blotted out.

In the sixth century, Benedict asked the monks in his order to make a vow of stability. At that time, *gyrovagues*—wandering monks— traveled from place to place, staying several days at a monastery, presumably until something displeased them (e.g., an annoying mannerism of a monk or the tedium of manual labor) and then left to travel again.[19] The term *gyrovague* combines the idea of "wandering" and "circles" to describe individuals who run in circles, lacking stability or commitment in their lives. "Always on the move," Benedict wrote, "they never settle down, and are slaves to their own wills and gross appetites."[20]

Today, many of us could also be classified as *gyrovagues*. Younger generations in particular like to keep their options open and tend to avoid long-term vocational commitments, regularly changing jobs and even careers. And many of us, when we confront irritation or difficulty in our work or our relationships, tend to seek out greener pastures. We may even feel a certain amount of "peace" about our decision, but that subjective sense of peace must be tested in prayer, against the Scriptures, and in healthy community. The peace that we feel in leaving behind a difficult or challenging situation may be a genuine gift from God, but it can also spring from a selfish sense of relief that comes from having less stress or fewer annoying people to deal with at work. Or our peace may be the result of the new comforts that come from having more money and influence, though this is not necessarily an indication that we are following God's will. As pilgrims of Christ, we must learn to discern whether an apparent consolation is from God ... or not.

In his book *Let Your Life Speak*, Parker Palmer describes how he had decided to accept the presidency of a college but wanted to give his decision an air of respectability by vetting it past a Quaker clearness committee, a circle of several trusted friends who help a person discern God's call by asking a series of honest questions. Palmer was certain the job was for him, until someone in the circle simply asked, "What would you like most about being a president?"

"Well, I would not like having to give up my writing and my teaching.... I would not like the politics of the presidency, never knowing who your real friends are.... I would not like having to glad-hand people I do not respect simply because they have money ..."

Gently but firmly, the person who had posed the question interrupted him: "I asked what you would most *like*?" "Yes, yes, I'm working my way toward an answer." Then he resumed his litany of complaints. Once again the questioner called him back to the original question. But this time he felt compelled to give the only honest answer he possessed, an answer that appalled him, even as he spoke it aloud: "Well ... I guess what I'd like most is getting my picture in the paper with the word *president* under it." After a respectful silence the questioner asked, "Parker, can you think of an easier way to get your picture in the paper?"

Palmer reflects, "By then it was obvious, even to me, that my desire to be president had much more to do with my ego than with the ecology of my life." He later conceded that, had he taken the job, it would have been bad for him and a disaster for the school.[21] Though it was less glamorous than the presidency of a college, and painful to his pride, Palmer decided to continue working in relative obscurity as a teaching fellow in a rural, wooded community in Maryland. But he wouldn't have been led to this decision on his own. The exercise of prayerful discernment and a willingness to give honest answers to trusted friends enabled him to discover and embrace how God was leading him to stay.

When we remain rooted in a particular workplace we have a unique opportunity to grow and change. Benedict was aware of the power of a lifelong vow of stability and how it could transform those who kept it. As another monk later explained: "[Benedict] introduced this vow [of stability] into his rule precisely because he knew that the limitations of the monk, and the limitations of the community he lived in, formed a part of God's plan for the *sanctification* both of individuals and of communities" (emphasis added).[22] As is true of other commitments, such as marriage with its own experiences of "for better" and "for worse," being committed to a group of people with their quirks and foibles over time serves as a furnace that reveals our selfishness and shortcomings and opens the way for us to grow and change. In these committed relationships, a person does not just keep a vow, the vow *keeps the person*.

As we weave prayer into the rhythm of our days, feel the joy of co-creating with God, and invite God to transform us through our work, then unlike my stockbroker friend who regretted not being able to retire at age forty, we will find ourselves daydreaming less about taking early retirement and savoring God more each day— not only in our rest but in our everyday work as well.

QUESTIONS FOR REFLECTION AND DISCUSSION

1. Ken's stockbroker friend yearned for early retirement. Why do many people view work as a kind of prison sentence from which they are seeking early escape?
2. In what ways do God the Father, Jesus, and the Holy Spirit ennoble work?
3. Do you see yourself co-creating with God in your work? If so, how?
4. How can your rhythm of prayer make you more conscious of God as you work at your company, school, or home?
5. How does offering our work to God shape the quality of our work?
6. Charlie and Don were guided by God in their work as they prayed. Have you ever had an experience where praying helped you discern God's will for your work?

WRITING YOUR RULE

Draft the basic boundaries of a work week you sense would honor God.

— CHAPTER 14 —

SENDING A RIPPLE THROUGH ETERNITY

I was sitting alone on one side of a long rectangular table in the board room of one of Tokyo's landmark corporate towers. It was my final job interview for a promising position in the company. Sitting on the other side of the table were four people: three managers and an administrative assistant seated off to the far right. The manager in the middle of the group was a man in his mid-fifties. He had a stout build, a square jaw, and a husky voice — a Japanese version of Jack Nicholson.

"If we hire you," he rasped, "how long would you stay with our company?"

I paused to consider his question. "Not that long. Maybe two or three years."

"Why not longer?" he asked me.

"One day, I hope to enter the Christian ministry. That's my long-term goal."

The manager furrowed his brow, leaned in, and growled, "Why would you want to do *that*?"

My heart began to beat faster and my mind went blank. I mumbled something along the lines of, "I think it would be the best way for me to serve people." It was the best I could do.

Riding home on the subway after the interview I reflected on that question and decided that my answer was incomplete. I wasn't interested in Christian ministry simply because I wanted to *serve people*; I wanted to do something with my life that would *last forever*. For me, this meant becoming a pastor.

Of course, you don't need to enter full-time pastoral ministry to make your life count. No matter what our gifts or calling, we all long to make the world a place of greater beauty and justice. We all yearn to do something meaningful, something that will last forever.

IT BEGINS AND ENDS WITH LOVE

The goal of any rhythm of spiritual practices is to immerse ourselves in the bottomless depth of God's love and from that place become people who truly love God and others. It is precisely because we are loved by God that we are able to offer love back to him and others. Loving God and loving people, of course, are closely connected. Jesus taught if we love God, we will love others and if we love people, we love God. Jesus said that when we feed the hungry, welcome the stranger, look after the sick, and visit the imprisoned—when we serve people—we are really serving him.[1]

St. Augustine defined sin as *incurvatus in se* or "turned in on oneself." This theological phrase describes sin as a life lived inwardly for the self rather than outwardly for God and others. When we experience the love of God, however, something in us lifts and straightens. Instead of living only for ourselves we begin to live for God and others. Again, the ability to love others and to love God finds its source in God's own love for us. Otherwise, "love" diminishes to duty, lessens to a lifeless chore. The great saints were not simply those who loved much; they were people who knew *they* were loved much by God. When we know how much we are cherished by our maker, we cannot help but overflow with love for others. A rule creates space for us to be with Jesus so that we enter into a deeper experience of God's love for us. One of the signs that we are truly united with Christ is that we have this sense of his love streaming into our hearts.[2] As his love wells up within us, we overflow with love for others.

After Hurricane Katrina devastated Louisiana, the United Way and MTV recruited one hundred volunteer students to help with the relief efforts during spring break. As wonderful as that is, a single

Christian organization was able to mobilize over *seven thousand* students to go and serve. A well-known journalist and politician, Roy Hattersley, was reporting on the relief efforts for the *UK Guardian* at the time. Hattersley, an atheist, observed that the support for those in need came overwhelmingly from Christian churches and organizations: "Notable by their absence were teams from rationalist societies and atheist associations." After watching the Salvation Army lead several other Christian organizations in their relief effort after Hurricane Katrina, Hattersley said, "It is an unavoidable conclusion that Christians are the most likely to make sacrifices involved in helping others."[3]

In fact, as we look back over Christian history, we see clear evidence of this leaning out to serve others. Like most of our personal family histories, Christian history also includes incidents that we as Christ followers are ashamed of, but there are vastly more stories of devotion and selfless service in the Spirit of Christ. We can be proud of dedicated Christians who have started orphanages, schools for impoverished children, shelters for the homeless, hospitals, and hospices. Followers of Christ have elevated the dignity and rights of women and advocated on behalf of slaves.

Christianity went viral in the first century largely because of the extraordinary way in which Christians reached out to others at a time when many people felt jaded and cynical. If you had walked past a garbage dump on the outskirts of a city in the Roman Empire during the first century, you would have likely seen discarded newborn babies left to die. We have letters from the ancient world in which parents were advised: "If it's a baby boy, keep it; if it's a girl, throw her away." Owners of slave houses would sometimes visit the garbage dumps and take discarded children and raise them to sell them as slaves. People who ran brothels would come and take away babies so they could one day be used as sex slaves. Christians came to the garbage dumps as well, but they would take the discarded children and raise them as their own.[4]

When Christians in the early centuries of the church lacked sufficient food for the hungry people at their door, the entire community would fast until they could share a meal together. It is estimated that in the year 250 in Rome, under Pope Cornelius, ten thousand Christians fasting a hundred days a year would have provided a million meals to the poor.[5] The world had never seen this kind of sacrificial love before. It was unexpected. Countercultural. Otherworldly.

In the early part of the fifth century, a sixteen-year-old boy named Patrick was living with his well-to-do family in England when he was kidnapped by pirates and carried off as a slave to what today is Ireland. For six years he herded pigs for a chieftain and suffered from hunger, thirst, and intense loneliness. In his suffering, Patrick began to pray and found solace through his new friendship with Christ. When he was twenty-two, Patrick was guided by a series of messages from God to walk through a forest and then along a coast to find a ship some two hundred miles away. Through this dramatic miraculous intervention, he was able to return to England and the safety of his parents. But Patrick did not stay long. He had a vision of a man from Ireland begging him to return, and Patrick responded by sailing back to Ireland — reentering the country where he had been trafficked into slavery, only now as a missionary. Once back, he launched a vigorous campaign against the common practice of slave trading, and through his influence, slavery in Ireland was eventually abolished, human sacrifice became unthinkable, and murder and intertribal warfare decreased.[6]

Some fourteen centuries later another remarkable figure named Amy Carmichael emerged from that same part of the world. She was born into a well-to-do family in North Ireland, but at age twenty-four she felt called by God to become a missionary. Robert Wilson, a respected clergyman who had become her adoptive father (after the death of her own father when she was eighteen), tried to dissuade her: "With your beauty and intelligence you'd be wasting your life by serving as a missionary." In spite of her health challenges (which caused her to be rejected as a missionary applicant with the China Inland Mission), Amy went on to serve for fifty-five years as a missionary in India — empowered and sustained in her work by a deep, intimate relationship with Christ. Although her days were long (from 5:00 a.m. until 10:00 p.m.), she and her missionary team organized the work day so that each hour they could pause and pray in response to a bell that was struck on the hour. They also had a practice of setting one day aside each month for prayer and seeking God.[7]

Amy's friendship with Christ compelled her to rescue girls and boys from temple prostitution. Parents in India who fell into financial destitution — then as now — had a habit of selling their infants into lifelong temple prostitution. Amy would often travel long distances on hot dusty roads to save one child. She battled in Indian courts to protect children. With the help of Indian Christian women, Amy rescued hundreds of these children: she clothed and fed them, shared Jesus with them, and educated them. Her more conservative Christian missionary colleagues criticized her, saying she should just stick with the more "spiritual" ministry of preaching the Bible. Amy Carmichael responded: "One cannot just save souls and pitchfork them to heaven. They are more or less fastened to bodies."

The examples of Patrick and Amy demonstrate that when we are filled with the Spirit of Christ, we are compelled to offer his love and justice to the forgotten and disenfranchised. In this way, the love of Christ is made visible to the world as we become the visible body of Christ on earth.[8] Saint Teresa of Avila said, "Christ has no body on earth but yours, no hands but yours, no feet but yours. Yours are the eyes through which Christ's compassion for the world is to look out; yours are the feet with which He is to go about doing good; and yours are the hands with which He is to bless us now."[9]

The Great Commandment begins with a call to love God and follows with a call to love our neighbor. As we have seen, these two commandments overlap, but they are in *sequence* for a reason. Love for our neighbor ideally flows from our love for God and his love for us. If we get the two reversed — trying to love others without receiving love from God — we will find ourselves running dry with nothing to give. As my seminary professor Haddon Robinson once said, "Before a ministry of service to others there must be a ministry to our spirit."[10] God must do something *in* us before we do something *for* him.

This is why prayer is such an essential part of service. In prayer we become more aware of God and his love for us and those around us. Even though Jesus — more than any other human being — enjoyed an intimate relationship with God the Father, before he began his active ministry he took time to deliberately savor the presence of his Father and revel in the knowledge that he was the beloved Son. Jesus, led by the Spirit, spent forty days praying and fasting in the desert before initiating his public ministry. After his ministry began, he also regularly withdrew to pray.[11] Jesus received God's *leading* and guidance through prayer. He spent a night praying in the hills before recruiting others to join him in his work.[12] Jesus also received *life* from his Father to do the work itself: "The words I say to you I do not speak on my own authority. Rather, it is the Father, living in me, who is doing his work."[13]

If this was true of Jesus, how much more do you and I need to experience the love of God through refreshing times of prayer and worship as the source of our service to others? The women and men who have been part of Mother Teresa's order have found their work sustainable across the years because each of them has a trellis of daily prayer that supports their life with and for God. Even amid the sounds of desperate people, blaring car horns, and street vendors selling their wares, they gather for regular times each day to still their bodies, minds, and spirits before the Lord in prayer. Mother Teresa's Sisters pray six hours a day and work five hours a day.[14] They also have a regular rhythm of rest—one day a week; one week a month; one month per year; one year in every six. Years ago, a friend of mine visited Mother Teresa in Calcutta and asked her, "With all the staggering needs in the world, how do you keep going?" She replied, "We pray the work: we do our work with Jesus, for Jesus, and to Jesus." Mother Teresa understood that her labor on behalf of the poor was more than anything else an expression of her devotion to Christ.[15]

PRAYER *IS* WORK

We need to change the way we think about prayer. Prayer is more than just the preparation for our service, an accessory for ministry, or a turbo charger that empowers us to do the "real work" of ministry. In a very real way, prayer is a work itself—it is *the* work of ministry. Prayer is a powerful force in shaping the world. When we pray, we resist the spiritual forces of evil that blind people. This is why the apostle Paul wrote: "Our struggle is not against flesh and blood, but ... against the spiritual forces of evil in the heavenly realm," calling us "to pray in the Spirit on all occasions" (Ephesians 6:12, 18).

Sean Litton, who serves with the nonprofit organization International Justice Mission (IJM), tells the story of a young woman, Elizabeth (not her real name),[16] who was enslaved in a brothel in northern Thailand. Lured by the promise of a good job, Elizabeth had been tricked into going to Thailand and forced to work as a sex slave. Members of International Justice Mission had been praying that God would intervene to cause the barriers to fall away so that they could offer assistance and aid to the girls who had been trafficked. In answer to their prayer they were able to cooperate with some local law enforcement officials (which was a miracle in itself), leading to the rescue of Elizabeth. After rescuing her, they discovered a small script scratched on the wall of the tiny room she had been locked inside. Sean asked a coworker to translate the characters for him into English. They read:

> The LORD is my light and my salvation—
>   so why should I be afraid?
> The LORD is my fortress, protecting me from danger,
>   so why should I tremble?
> When evil people come to devour me,
>   when my enemies and foes attack me,
>   they will stumble and fall.
> Though a mighty army surrounds me,
>   my heart will not be afraid.
> Even if I am attacked,
>   I will remain confident.

The team learned that Elizabeth was a Christ follower with a heart to serve God. She had written those words on the wall of her room as a visible reminder of her daily prayer for God to rescue her from the brothel. When Sean heard the words of Scripture being read he was stunned to realize that out of all the thousands of young girls being trafficked into Thailand, he and his team had rescued the one who had been specifically praying to God for deliverance. Overcome by the mercy and kindness of God, Sean broke down and wept. In spite of all of the challenges they had faced, the barriers and the complexity of working with the local officials, God had led them to Elizabeth—a clear answer to their prayer and hers.

In mysterious ways that we don't fully understand, God uses our prayers to heal and transform the world. Prayer is an act of reverence, but as Karl Barth has noted, it is also an act of defiance against the way things are.[17] In prayer we rise against the order of this age and join the transformation of the kingdom of this broken world to the kingdom of our Lord (Revelation 11:15).

Our praying doesn't have to begin in a chapel or a cave. It can rise spontaneously when we are exposed to someone's suffering. As we pray in response to a need we see, a new vision may rise within us. When my friend David Gotts was nineteen he was working as a junior banker in England. At the invitation of a friend, he donned a backpack to China with a charitable but ambiguous aim: to help those in need. David visited an orphanage, and he walked into a large room filled with cribs. Looking down into the first crib, he expected to see a cute little baby, but instead saw five babies jammed into the crib sideways. He thought that the babies would seek eye contact with him, but they were so malnourished and emaciated they lay there like lifeless rag dolls. Still reeling from that sight, David entered another room in a hidden part of the orphanage. Behind that door, he witnessed something no one should ever see, let alone experience: three little girls who had starved to death and another little girl who was literally within an hour of dying.

"I went to my hotel room that night," David said, "and I sat down and tried to understand what I had seen. I tried to make sense of it. I prayed, 'Why are children born into such pain and suffering?' "

He pleaded, "Where is your church, God? Where are the people who will go and help these children in China?" Then a small voice seemed to whisper to him, "David, *you* are here. What will you do?" Like Moses, David doubted that he could do anything. "Who am I, God? Why would you send me? I am not a doctor or a nurse or a development person. I have no skills. What could *I* do? And, God, I don't want to live in the midst of suffering. I don't want to live with children dying around me. Send someone else." For eight months David wrestled in prayer. Though part of him still felt intimidated and did not want to go, he sensed a growing confirmation — a deepening sense of peace that God was calling him to do something to help orphaned children in China. One morning he said to himself, "I am inadequate. I am not the best choice to go and do this kind of work, but God is asking me to take up a challenge and I trust that he has not made a mistake."

In 1993, David founded International China Concern, a Christian development organization that builds homes for children who have nowhere else to go. These homes have become communities of love, hope, and opportunity for hundreds of China's disabled and abandoned. As with David, when we are exposed to a need and respond by praying, an unexpected vision may emerge for us too. Our call may not be as dramatic as his, but as we see a need and pray, God may also birth a vision in us to serve.

Once we have been exposed to a need and sense God leading us in some way, the next natural step is to respond to this new vision. This might mean giving financially or helping to raise funds. It could also be a response to a single individual — sponsoring a child or befriending someone who lives on the margins. All these actions may seem small, but they can make a big difference in the life of another person. These small acts of serving can also more easily become part of the natural fabric of our lives.

Not long ago, the *Vancouver Sun* ran a front-page story about a homeless young man named Thomas and a woman named Sherrill, a member of our faith community. According to the article, Thomas lived in front of London Drugs, a pharmacy in an upscale part of Vancouver. At night he slept in the back alley behind the store. He is not sure, but he believes he was born in Winnipeg. He does not know who his father is. His mother, who was addicted to drugs, abandoned him when he was just five months old.

Thomas went on to live in a series of foster homes where he was both physically and sexually abused. When he was just seven years old, he was introduced to cocaine by one of his foster parents. By age eight, he started using heroin. When he was thirteen, he ran away from his foster home and has lived on the streets ever since. Eventually Thomas came to Vancouver, and shortly after arriving met Sherrill. Sherrill often shopped at London Drugs, and when she saw Thomas outside the store, she would stop briefly to chat.

One day Sherrill asked Thomas: "What do you really want in life?"

"I want to get off the streets," he replied.

"Really?"

"Yes. *Really.*"

Sherrill began driving Thomas to his doctors' appointments. She picked him up when he got arrested. She gave him gift cards for food and helped him find a place indoors to live. She even started a small trust fund for him. (One of the donors is Sherrill's fourteen-year-old son, who donates ten dollars a month from his allowance.) Still, Thomas struggled with his addiction and Sherrill often wondered if her efforts were making any difference. And yet, five years after they met, Thomas's life had changed in significant ways. He had moved to a recovery house and begun attending AA and NA meetings regularly. Though he was already twenty-seven years old, Thomas decided to enroll as a freshman in high school. Referring to Sherrill, Thomas says: "She's my angel ... she is the thing that God sent me to believe."[18]

These stories may encourage us, but with so many needs right around us and in the larger world, we often become so overwhelmed that we end up doing nothing at all. How can we realistically weave justice into our rule of life?

CHOOSE ONE THING

Mike Yankoski is someone I know who is deeply committed to make the world a better place. He once voluntarily spent five months living as a homeless person to better understand their suffering.

I once asked Mike, "Can you give me some advice on how I can better work for justice in the world?"

He replied, "Choose *one* thing to focus on. For me and Danae [his wife] it's providing clean water for communities in the developing world."

Choose *one* thing to focus on. Wise counsel.

For me it is advocating on behalf of impoverished children in the developing world through sponsoring children and projects, fundraising, and serving as a trustee for World Vision.*

As you expose yourself to need and pray, your "one thing" may emerge. It might be human trafficking, HIV-AIDS, alleviating global debt for poor nations, housing for the poor, education, care for creation, or some other cause.

As you discover your "one thing," consider a specific way you can serve this cause as part of your rule of life.

When we serve we experience joy and find ourselves drawn closer to God, but there will also be times when our efforts feel like a drop in an ocean of human need. Remember, Scripture tells us that our work will not be in vain (1 Corinthians 15:58). Nothing done with and for Christ in this present time will be wasted in God's future. It will find its way into the new world. In Revelation 21:5 (NASB) God says, "I am making all things new." God does not say, "I will make all *new things*," but "I will make *all things new*." God tells us that he will renew the earth. Just as there will be continuity between our present bodies and our resurrected bodies in the world to come, there will also be continuity between this present earth and a new earth to come. The good we do on this earth will one day be remembered and magnified in the new world.

If our current world will be renewed at the coming of Christ, then what we do now—praying, giving, sponsoring children, building orphanages, digging wells, welcoming the homeless, caring for the earth, sharing the good news of the kingdom of Jesus Christ, and campaigning for justice—will last forever. In the words of author N. T. Wright, "These activities are not simply ways of making the present life a little less beastly, a little more bearable until the day we

* The net advance and royalty money for this book will go to support children and missions in Asia and Africa.

leave it behind altogether. They are part of what we may call *building for the kingdom.*[19] Wright continues, "You are not oiling the wheels of the machine that's about to roll over a cliff. You are not restoring a great painting that's shortly going to be thrown on the fire. You are not planting roses in a garden that's about to be dug up for a building site. You are, strange though it may seem, almost hard to believe as the resurrection itself, accomplishing something that will become in due course part of God's new world."[20] If this is true, then every prayer, every act of love and kindness, every minute spent teaching a special needs child to read or walk or listening to a lonely elderly person, every work of art or music inspired by the love of God, every act of care for the earth, every act that spreads the good news of the gospel, will find its way into the new creation that God is making and will one day bring to glorious completion.

QUESTIONS FOR REFLECTION AND DISCUSSION

1. Ken described how his job interview helped him realize that he yearned to do something that would last forever. Have you ever had an experience in which you became powerfully aware of your desire to make a lasting difference?

2. Like most of our family histories, there are stories from church history that Christ followers should be ashamed of, but there are many more stories about which we can feel a healthy sense of pride. What are some of those inspiring stories for you?

3. Why is prayer so central to our work for God? In what sense is prayer *the* work? How does Jesus model dependence on God through prayer during his ministry?

4. Have you ever had a vision for a work of God rising in your heart? What was it? How did you respond?

5. Do you have a sense as to what "one thing" you might commit yourself to?

WRITING YOUR RULE

As your "one thing" emerges, draft how you might serve this work of God, using a specific time frame (monthly, quarterly, yearly).

— CHAPTER 15 —

SHARING THE PRESENCE

Our three-year-old son Joey loves spare ribs. On my day off when I pick up Joey from his preschool he will excitedly say to me, "Ribs! Ribs! I want ribs." So, for the last few months we've been in the habit of going to Earls, a local restaurant, and getting take-out ribs for dinner. On a recent Monday, I walked into Earls with Joey to pick up our order and the hostess told me that the manager, a woman named Rachel, wanted to meet with me. Rachel came out to where we were waiting and said, "I've noticed that you've been coming in every Monday with your son to pick up ribs. As a way to say thank you, your dinner today is on us." She handed me a box of ribs and on the box I saw written: "Thank you for your business on Monday nights." A big heart was drawn beneath those words and it was signed "Rachel and the Earls team."

I was blown away. First of all, I was surprised by the fact that she even remembered us. Earls is a sit-down restaurant and we rarely come to the restaurant to eat, preferring to order take-out. But I was also touched by her act of kindness. Driving home, I called my wife and told her what happened. Later that evening, I called my sister in Montreal, who had worked as a waitress in high school, and told her the story.

When something good happens to us, even if it's a relatively small thing, we tell people about it. When it's something big—getting accepted to college, receiving a promotion at work, becoming engaged, adopting a baby—we naturally want to share the good news with other people. In a similar way, as we draw close to Christ and more deeply grasp how kind he has been to us, we will naturally want to share the good news of what he has done for us with others.

UP AND OUT

As we saw in the opening chapter, as Celtic monks drew close to God in the sixth century, they intentionally built their monasteries close to the "world"—near settlements; on well-known hilltops, or on islands by established sea-lanes—so that they could reach out to people with the hospitality of Christ. The monasteries not only provided a place of prayer but also served as hotels, emergency shelters, hospitals, libraries, universities, centers for the arts, and mission-sending bases.

Although our values will differ from those of mainstream society, as we are guided by the Spirit we will not withdraw from the world or disconnect from people who don't know the living God. Just as Christ was sent by his Father into the world, when we are in Christ and Christ is in us, we will seek to obey him by being "in the world, but not of the world" (see John 17:13–19).

The television show *GCB* (originally based on the provocatively titled novel *Good Christian Bitches*) is a parody of Christianity in the Bible Belt South. While the program uses satire, we are aware of how some churchgoers can gossip, conspicuously consume, and live with a superficiality that rivals the people of the "world." As the show suggests, it is possible to be in the church but continue to be *of* the world, having the same values as the world we disdain yet ironically avoid, isolated in our Christian enclave. But this is not the authentic fruit of following Christ. As we become more deeply united with Christ and more of his character is reflected in ours, we will find that while our values are distinct from those of our culture, we nonetheless genuinely love those who do not know Jesus. Like Jesus, we will find that we are the "friend of sinners," enjoying the company of people who do not believe in the living God.

An important first step in becoming people who share the gospel is to pray for people around us who don't know Christ and to trust God to work in their lives. As we turn to God in prayer, we are reminded that God is preeminent in all of this, preparing people's hearts to receive him. Communicating Christ is not primarily about our competencies; it is something the Holy Spirit does through us.

Sabine is a graduate student in our faith community who conducted scientific research in Antarctica with an international team of students and professors. For a variety of reasons, she sensed that conversations about faith were not particularly likely, but one evening she prayed that God would give her colleagues an indication of the true Master behind the creation they were all studying. She shared:

> The next day we hiked up to a summit overlooking Paradise Bay, fittingly named for its mirror-smooth waters surrounded by glistening snow-covered glaciers and the setting sun. I'd never seen such compelling evidence in nature for the goodness of creation and the greatness of its Creator. We observed the scene in silence, and that evening the atmosphere on the boat was quiet and reflective. During our evening debrief our expedition leader, who had reminded us daily about the importance of good karma, commented quietly that our experience could only have been attributed to a higher power. Quite taken aback by his statement, I was even further moved when another staff member, a burly, joking man, stood before the group seemingly at a loss for words. He finally said that, though he had never before considered himself religious, he had encountered such a profound and overwhelming sense of spiritual connection it had to be divine. God met our research team powerfully that day through the sheer beauty of his creation. Sometimes all we are asked to do is to pray and experience life with others.

Knowing the Holy Spirit is opening a person's heart to God— whether through the beauty of creation, someone's kindness, or an affliction of some sort—takes the pressure off our shoulders.

THE MYSTERIOUS WORK OF GOD

When I was new to the Christian faith and just beginning to share the gospel I was concerned about having to say things the right way and getting through a four-point outline. While God certainly can and does use simple bullet-point outlines, I now see conversion as more of a mysterious work of God in the life of a person, something that begins long before I arrive and continues long after I'm out of the picture. This was certainly true with my friend Nathan.

Nathan had been a successful stockbroker but found that the business world left his soul empty. As a teenager he had been recognized as a gifted artist and had been admitted to one of Canada's finest art schools, but because of financial difficulties he chose to pursue a business career instead. Now, after successfully establishing himself in business, he had decided to leave the business world and, to use his words, "follow his bliss." Nathan turned to Buddhist writings, yet he sensed a yearning for something else. Through a friend, he was introduced to our church, and after about a year, his friend and the people in our church community helped him see that God's hand was upon him and that he was being drawn to Jesus. Nathan's ventures in the business world had revealed his inner emptiness. His pursuit of beauty through art and his dabbling in Buddhism prepared him to see his need for Jesus.

The doctrine of prevenient grace teaches that God is at work in a person's life long before there are any visible signs that they are being drawn to God. The word *prevenient* literally means "come before" (from the Latin *prae*, "before" and *venire*, *vent*, "come"). God's grace precedes conversion, "coming before" a person ever makes a conscious decision to seek God (John 6:44). In fact, our yearning for God is itself a gift from God. The great theologian Jonathan Edwards viewed authentic conversion as something God was doing to people, rather than something they initiated. In this sense, conversion was more a recognition of God's sovereign grace at work, rather than a "decision" a person made for Jesus.[1] This means that our primary role, as those who communicate the gospel, is to serve not as a salesperson but as a hiking guide. We aren't trying to convince people that they should follow God; we are helping them see the work of God that is already in their lives. There is less of an emphasis on "closing the deal" and more on simply being a friend on the journey, observing the beauty of God's grace in their lives.

UP FOR THE CALL?

Despite this understanding of God's grace, for many of us the thought of sharing our faith with another person is still intimidating. We feel under-qualified, ill-equipped. We don't want to come across as a pushy "televangelist." I'm comforted to know that even the famous ambassador for Jesus, Billy Graham, describes feeling a twinge of fear — even into his later years — whenever a conversation with a friend who is not a believer turns to spiritual matters. We may experience pushback at times because of our faith, and Jesus said that such resistance to our witness should be expected: "If they persecuted me, they will persecute you also."[2]

I have a longtime friend who doesn't believe in a personal God. For him "god" is nature, the great outdoors — which he encounters through mountain biking. Occasionally, when I speak of God he says to me, "You have your beliefs and I have mine." I know he's not trying to upset me, but I still feel a pang of rejection. Our conversation is momentarily awkward until we move on to another topic. Many of us have felt that uncomfortable fear when it comes time to talk about our faith. But because the Spirit is at work around us, we will also experience times when sharing our faith is natural. Several times I have felt the unexpected peace and joy that "surpasses understanding" when sharing my faith with another person. It isn't always this way — but it does affirm to me that the Spirit works through us.

THE FOUR SIDES OF THE GOSPEL

So how do we practically go about sharing our faith? One of the most helpful pictures of sharing Jesus with others comes from Bryant Myers, a former vice president of World Vision International. Bryant often says that when sharing the gospel in a different culture, particularly with those who may oppose the Christian message, it is helpful to see the gospel as a four-sided pyramid: *life, deed, sign,* and *word.*[3]

Depending on the context and the leading of the Holy Spirit, you might choose a particular side of the gospel to lead with and, as opportunity allows, progress to sharing all "sides" of the gospel. The ideal is to eventually share the gospel as an organic whole that encompasses life, deed, sign, and word.

World Vision, for example, does relief and development work in countries where governments do not allow them to speak to people about Christ. In places such as these, it's not likely that a person will *begin* communicating the gospel by word but through life, deed, or sign. Even in places like North America or Europe, which are considered largely "Christian," people have such a wide variety of beliefs that the four-sided pyramid metaphor of the gospel is helpful.

I realize that describing the gospel as life, deed, sign, and word is somewhat abstract, so let's take a moment to unpack each component.

LIFE

One of the most visible ways that we share the gospel with others is through our lives. The example of a life transformed by Christ can serve as compelling proof of the reality of God. The apostle Paul exhorts us, as followers of Christ, to live our lives in such an attractive way that people who don't believe are drawn into a friendship with the living God.[4] As we are guided by our rule of life, we should find ourselves becoming more like Jesus, and as this happens, consciously or unconsciously, we will be commending Christ to people around us through the way we live. Communicating the gospel in this way is often a necessary prelude to sharing it through our words—particularly with those who may oppose it.

My grandfather, a powerful, arrogant corporate CEO, was generally hostile to Christians. (When I was working in Japan, I gave him a copy of *Mere Christianity* by C. S. Lewis that had been translated into Japanese. He had his secretary reduce the entire book to a one-page summary!) There was one person in his company, however, whom he described with a gleam in his eye as a "true Christian." This person had extraordinary integrity and was truly conscientious and trustworthy. I don't know if this man ever tried to persuade my grandfather to become a follower of Christ. He was simply open about his faith to the point where my grandfather and the others at work knew he was a Christian. My grandfather deeply respected him. In fact, part of the reason my grandfather later committed his life to Christ—at age eight-six—was because of this man whose character testified to the reality of Christ.

As we experience the transforming power of Jesus Christ in our lives, people will be drawn to know more about the God who is at work in us. Kim lived near our home and preferred a New Age style of spirituality. Compassionate by nature, she was impressed by our church's commitment to the homeless and volunteered with us even though she wasn't a follower of Jesus. She was attracted to Christ, but she had trouble with the idea that Christ was a unique way to God. Some time ago, she sent me a birthday card and wrote something I'll always remember. I don't know the details of her spiritual commitment, but in the card she wrote me these words: "I thank God that he brought someone in my life that I could trust enough to lead me to Christ." We don't have to be perfect to manifest the visible fruit of the Holy Spirit: love, joy, peace, patience, kindness, goodness, gentleness, and self-control (see Galatians 5:22–23). If Christ is at our core, he will radiate through our lives *before* we've even said a thing about him.

DEED

This leads to a second way we can communicate the gospel — through our *deeds*. Life and deed, of course, are linked, but when I speak of communicating the gospel through "life" the focus is *character*, whereas in "deed" the focal point is *action*.

Where do we find this idea in Scripture? Jesus said that as his followers we should let our light shine before others in such a way that they will see our good *deeds* and become more open to God.[5] In Acts 4 we see this idea in action as we read how the early followers of Christ shared their possessions with one another so that there was not a single person in need among them. Their sacrificial actions *prompted questions*, which in turn opened the door for those who knew Christ to proclaim the gospel through their words. Sharing the gospel through deeds is an especially powerful way to share Christ in places where people are not initially receptive to hearing about Jesus.

"Several years ago," a young Cambodian man shared, "World Vision came to my community and set up a TB clinic to care for those suffering with that disease. They helped us improve our schools, and taught us better farming methods to increase our crop yields. Since the genocide in Cambodia, I did not trust strangers. I was suspicious of the World Vision people. 'Why would these strangers help us?' I wondered. One day I confronted the World Vision leader and demanded to know, 'Why are you here?' The leader said, 'We are followers of Jesus Christ, and we are commanded to love our neighbors as ourselves.'" The Cambodian asked, "Who is Jesus?" The workers at World Vision gave him a Bible and later introduced him to a Cambodian Christian. Eventually, this man became a follower of Jesus and a pastor of a church. Today, Pastor Ourng serves a church of eighty-three members in Cambodia.

Demonstrating love in practical ways prompts questions from

people in developing countries who live with staggering poverty, but also from middle-class people in North America whose heart needs are just as great. Rose is an active member of our Tenth community. She met her friend Patti twenty-eight years ago when Rose's daughter and Patti's son were born at British Columbia (BC) Women's Hospital on the same day. Six years later Patti and her family moved three houses down from Rose and her family. They ended up becoming close friends for more than twenty years.

Then, four years ago Patti was diagnosed with cancer in her appendix. The cancer spread into her abdomen and then into her spine. For about five months, as Patti's need for care became acute, Rose organized friends to spend the day with her at the hospital, which gave Patti's husband a much-needed break.

Rose herself was at Patti's bedside in the palliative care unit along with Patti's husband Chris near the end. As the pain came in intense waves and they knew she was close to dying, Rose stroked her head and arms, praying for her. She whispered to her friend: "It's okay. It's okay. It's okay to go … you're going to a better place."

Soon afterward, Patti died. While Patti had placed her faith in Christ many years ago, her husband Chris was still not a believer in God. After seeing the care and love his wife had received from Rose and the other members of our church, Chris was moved to investigate Christ for himself. He shared with me, "I knew *then* that they were in touch with a reality of which I knew nothing about and thought, 'What am I missing?'" Seeing the love that Rose had for Patti and the faith both of them had in the reality of God made Chris think that there was something he was missing in his own life. Rose and her husband invited Chris to our church, where he has been attending for the past two years. Recently, Chris took his first communion with us at Tenth.

Our actions sometimes speak louder than our words, and they can powerfully testify to the reality of God, opening the door for an opportunity to share the good news about Jesus.

SIGN

The early church, filled with the Holy Spirit, often bore witness to Christ and his power through signs and miraculous works. When

Jesus was ministering among skeptics, the miraculous signs he performed would encourage people to take a step toward belief.[6] In the book of Acts we see how the early believers also experienced certain "signs" that could only be plausibly explained by God: the ability to speak in tongues they hadn't studied before, healings, and supernatural deliverances from danger.

When we are joined to Christ and filled with his Spirit, we will also bear witness to the reality of God through some kind of "sign" of God's power at work in our lives. My family's spiritual heritage began with a sign. I was born in a country where most people are Buddhist or Shinto. The Christian stream of our family began with my great uncle who was diagnosed with tuberculosis at a time when it was considered a terminal illness. There was no medication for him to take and he was given six months to live. A missionary gave him a Bible and prayed that he would come to know Jesus personally. He read the Bible and came to the part in the Gospels where Jesus was healing people. My great uncle prayed for healing and was miraculously healed. He ended up living to a ripe old age (when he was in his seventies I played golf with him). As a result of his healing, he came to Christ and eventually led my mother to faith in Christ as well. And as a result of my mother's influence, I too came to know Christ.

My friend Aisyah's spiritual journey also began with a sign from God. Aisyah was born in a Muslim country in a family that can trace its lineage back to the prophet Muhammad. Her parents were committed to raising her as a dedicated Muslim and so she faithfully went to the mosque, prayed, fasted during Ramadan, and made holy pilgrimages.

However, when it was time for Aisyah to go to university, her parents sent her to a small Christian college in the United States since one of the professors was a friend of the family. Feeling at a disadvantage in the one required Bible class, Aisyah approached a Christian friend to teach her what the Bible was all about. As she studied the Bible, she was first introduced to the teachings of Jesus Christ.

One day, her friend challenged Aisyah to pray and ask the Jesus of the Gospels to reveal himself to her. She agreed to the challenge with one condition: her friend must ask the same of Allah. Aisyah began to question her own Islamic faith for the first time in her life, and she imagined what would happen if she actually *did* come to believe in Jesus. Would her family disown her? Afraid of such consequences, Aisyah stopped hanging out with her Christian friends. After a couple of months, she thought the stirrings in her heart were gone. But one weekend, when her roommate had gone home, Aisyah had an unusual experience in the middle of the night—she encountered the risen Jesus. "I either dreamed this or someone did actually come to the room and simply said, 'Trust me.' Years later I discovered that my experience was very similar to those of many Muslims who have experienced God showing himself to them in a dream. It's so amazing that the God of the universe would do such a thing! Wow!" The following morning she went to her friend and told him that she had been visited by Jesus. He asked her if she wanted to follow Christ and allow him to be the leader in her life ... and she said yes.

Of course, not every sign of God's reality is as dramatic as a healing or a vision. A number of people throughout church history have begun their spiritual pilgrimage simply after experiencing a powerful sense of love and well-being. A stockbroker in Houston went through a major failure in his professional life. A strong, high-achieving person, he found himself reduced to tears in his study during the middle of this crisis. When his tears abated and his vision cleared, he saw his own hands folded in the shape of a church building, something he had learned as a little child in Sunday school. It had been many decades since he'd attended a church, but that simple sign amidst his grief impacted him profoundly. It was a holy moment. In the weeks that followed, he set out to find the nearest church so that he could seek God again. He ended up coming to my friend Jacob's church and grew significantly in his faith.

Signs and wonders are not just an experience of the early church, something God used in the book of Acts. Today, the Holy Spirit continues to give people signs that help point them to Christ. As we draw closer to Christ through our rule of life and are filled with the Spirit of Jesus, we may find ourselves sharing him with others through miraculous signs as well.

WORD

The gospel is an organic whole encompassing evidence of life change, deeds of loving service to others, miraculous signs, and words that testify to the living Jesus. As we express the whole gospel, at some point we will use our words. With stark simplicity Paul asks, "How can people trust in a Christ they have never heard of?"[7] Words help us make clear the source of our life change, the motivation for our deeds, and the power behind the signs. Our lives and deeds alone are never enough to fully communicate the gospel. There are people who may say that they do not need to make a vocal witness, because their lives say all that needs to be said, but while this appears humble, it is naive. No single life alone can adequately articulate the gospel.[8]

I remember hearing the respected Christian leader Bill Bright share a story about an upright Christian man who decided he would just preach the gospel with his life. One of his colleagues approached him and said, "Bob, I've noticed there's something different about you" (and Bob thought, *Praise God, the strategy has worked!*). "You're not like the rest of us ..." (Bob thought, *Lord, this is my moment!*) "There is something unique about you ..."

"Bob, are you a vegetarian?"

It is necessary for us to express the gospel in words, if only to avoid confusion.

Sharing our faith through our words doesn't have to be complicated. If our friendship with Jesus Christ is an important and growing part of our lives, it should be natural for us—and honoring to him—to speak of our love for Jesus. Some time ago, I was at a dinner with a small group of people hosted by a prominent city leader who had received the Order of Canada, the highest government award bestowed on a civilian in our country. The host asked each of us at the table to share for five minutes something that we were really passionate about. As other people were speaking, I was half listening to them and half thinking about what I would say.

A part of me wanted to talk about my love of running through the woods with our golden retriever or sailing. But I realized that my greatest passion is my relationship with Jesus Christ. Still, I hesitated because I thought talking about this might not go over well with this group. When it was my turn to share, I took a deep breath and said, "I am a Christian minister; I serve as the pastor of Tenth Church here in Vancouver. When people learn that I once worked in the business world, they wonder why I would ever choose the somewhat unusual vocation of a Christian minister. When I was a teenager, I went through some rebellious years. I got into shoplifting, using and selling drugs on a small scale, and temporarily borrowing other people's cars—without their knowing it. My dad, a conservative Asian man, experienced great stress over my actions. He took me on a 'field trip' to a local prison and said to me, 'I just wanted to see your future home ... room and board courtesy of my tax dollars.' Unfortunately, I wasn't 'scared straight.' My dad had just become a follower of Jesus Christ, and so he decided on a different strategy. He took me to a Christian youth conference. At that conference I heard for the first time that through a relationship with Jesus Christ I could have a new beginning. I intuitively knew that I was headed in the wrong direction and so when the speaker gave us an opportunity to pray, I offered all that I knew of me to all that I knew of Jesus. Looking back at my life, I see that as the most powerful, transformative moment of my life. I am now a pastor because I want to be part of a community where people can experience the wonder of a life-changing friendship with Jesus." Then I turned to the person on my left and said, "Next."

Later on, the young woman who was providing the after-dinner singing entertainment paused before one of her numbers and asked the host if she could also share briefly. Our host nodded. "It's interesting that Ken is here," she said. "For the last six months or so I've been attending Ken's church and just about a month ago I also committed my life to Christ at Tenth through baptism. And it's made all the difference."

It felt like a holy moment.

When Christ is at work in our lives, we will naturally want to share our story as the Holy Spirit gives us opportunity. And when we speak, other Christ followers may become emboldened to speak as well. Sharing our story is often one of the most natural and powerful ways we testify to the reality of Christ. As we draw closer to Christ, we will find that sharing him with others will not feel so much like an obligation but rather something that overflows from our inner joy.

When I worked in Tokyo, I began to preach occasionally at my small church. The pastor was eighty years old and was looking for someone to pinch-hit for him from time to time. As I anticipated one day going to seminary and entering pastoral ministry, I eagerly volunteered for this opportunity. When my grandmother heard a rumor that I would be preaching one weekend, she was both intrigued and amused. She remembered me as a little brat whose favorite book was the Sears Christmas catalog and she recalled that I always used to ask her, "Grandma, how can I be rich when I grow up?" More out of curiosity than anything else, she decided she would come and hear me preach. She had not been to church in over two decades. On a cold, wet February morning, she rode the Tokyo subway and buses for over an hour to come to our church.

My grandmother sat in the second to last row on the right hand side of our small chapel. I got up and gave a short message on the work of the cross from Galatians 2 and then sat down. Our pastor came to the podium and offered this critique: "Brother Shigematsu, after that kind of message, you should have given an invitation." He continued, "Come up here and give an invitation ..."

I was unprepared and embarrassed. The mood in the chapel grew tense and awkward. I had recently watched Billy Graham on video so I plagiarized him. I said, "If you are here and don't know Christ, if you need to make your commitment or recommitment to Christ, I want you to stand up and come. By coming you're saying in your heart, 'I commit myself to Jesus.'" As we sang the closing hymn, I looked up after the first stanza and saw no one coming. My heart sank. We sang the second stanza and still no one moved. I began thinking whatever special anointing or charisma Christian ministers are supposed to have, I certainly didn't have *it*. After the third stanza, one woman shuffled like a mouse to the aisle and toward the front (I knew that she was already a Christian and was likely coming forward only because she felt sorry for me and wanted to encourage me by walking down the aisle). We sang the final stanza and I closed the hymnal.

But when I looked up again, to my astonishment there were

nearly twenty people up front—and my grandmother was among them! Tears were streaming down her face. I jumped off the platform and asked her, "Are you okay?" She said, "This is the happiest day of my life. I thought I was a Christian, but today for the first time I understood why Jesus Christ died on the cross for me." I think of that day as one of the greatest days of my life, because it was the day my grandmother experienced peace with God. When we point someone to Christ it may not be our grandmother, but it's somebody's grandmother, somebody's son, somebody's daughter, somebody's sister, somebody's dad … somebody's "somebody."

As followers of Christ, we not only have the privilege of deepening our friendship with him through our rule but the joy of pointing people through our life, deeds, signs, and words to the only One who can satisfy the deepest longings of their souls.

QUESTIONS FOR REFLECTION AND DISCUSSION

1. As was true of Sabine in Antarctica and of my friend Nathan the artist, have you ever sensed God's prevenient grace at work (that is, where God was at work in a person's life before they *consciously* believed)?

2. How can this knowledge of God's prevenient grace free us from fear or insecurity as we bear witness to the reality of God?

3. Even Billy Graham describes feeling a twinge of fear whenever a conversation with a friend who is not a believer turns to spiritual matters. Have you ever felt awkwardness (or pushback) when sharing your faith with someone else? If so, how did you deal with the awkwardness?

4. What, according to Bryant Myers, are the four sides of the gospel pyramid? Which side is easiest for you to share? Which side is most difficult for you to share?

WRITING YOUR RULE

Describe a simple regular practice you could engage in that would help you faithfully bear witness to Christ.

AFTERWORD

Perhaps I was having an unusually good day or something happened that made me feel especially grateful ... I can't remember.
But, not long ago my wife said, "You're the happiest pastor I know."
(Remember, she was born and raised in Japan and she doesn't know
many pastors — and if you happen to be a pastor, she likely doesn't
know you.)

Afterward, I thought to the extent that I feel happiness and experience joy, it's largely because I am blessed with a loving family and a
supportive team at Tenth. These gifts make a huge difference.

But, my happiness also largely flows from my rule of life, this
trellis that supports my friendship with God.

I used to feel like I was always treading water and sometimes
feared I'd drown under a tidal wave of work and responsibility.
Thanks to my rule, I now enjoy the life-imparting gift of the Sabbath
and a simpler, less cluttered life. I thus live from a place of greater rest
and peace than I would otherwise. I don't lead an idyllic existence.
I'm busy. In my line of work, I face crisis after crisis. But, rarely do I
feel overwhelmed by life.

I am the kind of guy who can become consumed by climbing the
proverbial ladders of success that are propped up against the wrong
walls. My rule also helps me keep first things first: God, my family,
and my vocation. That's not to say that I haven't failed or don't have
regrets. I have and I do. But my rule clarifies what's most important
in life and spurs me to take *action* around first things. For example,
even in chaotic times, my rule supports a simple rhythm of prayer

that helps me stay more conscious of Christ throughout the day, weaving friendship with God into my work, family life, exercise, and play—God in my everything. And perhaps this is why people have remarked, "You seem content" or "You're holding your work with open hands."

My life of service once felt like I was drawing from a dry well, scraping for something scarce. I now feel like the water line in my reservoir has risen to a healthy level. The gifts of friendship with God and people help me to drink from the source of Living Water. On discouraging days—which I still of have plenty of—my rule helps me put one foot in front of the other, and on good days it empowers me to run and mount up on wings like eagles.

Happiness is not the goal of the rule, but joy and peace and love are the fruit of a life rooted in Christ—and our trellis supports this relationship.

The pattern of daily life fostered by a rule may sound simple, but it can and will shape the whole of our lives. Annie Dillard reminds us that the *way we live our days* is the *way we live our lives*.

So may the Spirit lead you to create a rule of life that frees you to enjoy the Sabbath rest of God and a flourishing friendship with Jesus, that empowers you to faithfully honor first things, and that sustains you in a life of service to God and others.

May you experience Christ in every part of your life.

God in your everything.

We began our journey in Ireland. As we close, let me take us back there one last time and offer you a blessing attributed to St. Patrick. This prayer reminds us that the goal of the rule is not the rule itself but Christ at the center of all that we are and do:

> May the strength of God pilot you,
> May the wisdom of God uphold you, and
> May the power of the Holy Spirit sustain you.
>
> May Christ be in on your right, Christ on your left,
> May Christ be in front of you,
> May Christ be behind you,

May Christ be under you, above you, and
May Christ be within you.

In the name of the Father, Son and Holy Spirit,
Amen.

APPENDIX:
SAMPLE RULES OF LIFE

I have described parts of my rule of life throughout the book. Here, consolidated in one place, is my rule as well as the rules of several other people in various ages and stages of life.

KEN'S RULE

Take a 24-hour Sabbath once a week

Begin each day with Scripture and prayer

Pray the *Examen* before going to sleep at night

Run 2–3x a week, swim 2x a week

Aim to be home by 5:15 p.m. each day, and to be home at least 4 evenings a week

Fast on Thursdays

Go on a date with my wife once every 2–3 weeks

Meet with a spiritual director once a month

Host people from different backgrounds in our home about once a month

Take a yearly spiritual retreat with my mentoring group

Take a yearly summer vacation with my family and spend New Year's in Japan with my wife's family

Tithe to my local church and give to impoverished children and missions in the developing world to the point where we feel financially stretched

BRITTANY'S RULE
(graduate student in her 20s)

On a daily basis I will:

- Spend time with God through Bible study, meditation or memorization, prayer or worship
- Focus on eating as healthy as possible (no wheat or dairy and minimal sugar) and getting at least 7–8 hours of sleep each night

On a weekly basis I will:

- Sabbath each Sunday
- Participate in church at the Sunday evening service and at young adults group on Monday night
- Spend quality time with my boyfriend (both play and recreation, as well as time in prayer)
- Spend quality time with my best friend (play, exercise, and recreation)
- Exercise 3–4 times a week

On a biweekly or monthly basis I will:

- Spend quality time with my parents and brother
- Tithe
- Connect with my peer-mentor/spiritual friend
- Reflect on how I'm meeting my goals/living my rule and where I need to grow

JUNE'S RULE
(married with young son, works as a teacher)

Sabbath:

• Rest and Sunday worship, typically on a Saturday or Sunday (depending on what's going on)

Prayer:

• As I can, pray throughout the day — in the car, on a walk, before mealtimes
• More concentrated times of prayer (1) when I put our toddler to bed and (2) before going to bed

Scripture reading:

• At night before I go to bed; as I can, pray through these Scriptures the following day

Spiritual friendship:

• Small group with families with young children (currently working through a Bible study book on parenting)

Recreation/play:

• Watch movies, favorite shows, dine out/in or hang out with friends/family, go to events/shows
• Travel once a year in the summertime

Care for the body:

• As I can, go for an hour jog once a week (if I'm lucky); this is hard in the winter and much easier in spring/summer
• Eat mostly at home so as to eat healthy

Family:

• Try to take our son to visit his grandparents once a week

Financial life:

• Tithe every month
• Support missionaries and other charitable organizations every month

Mission:

- Volunteer as a family at the local seniors' home once every 2 months
- Volunteer at camp each summer

Witness:

- Through friendship and invite people to church and through our Easter and Christmas outreaches

STEPHEN'S RULE
(in his 30s, married with young children, NGO worker Brazil)

Spiritual disciplines:

- Do morning devotional over breakfast after shower
- Finish evening with the *Examen*
- Invest in spiritual friendships in and outside Brazil

Mind and focus:

- Invest first fruits of my time and energy on spiritual life and creative work
- Email and Internet in afternoon and evening only

Work:

- Enjoy people daily, even brief connections
- Invest through my gifts: teach, lead, connect
- Immerse in Brazilian culture: reading, radio, TV, movies
- Review action list daily, set goals for next day

Finances:

- Steward funds well, especially giving and investing

Marriage and family:

- Serve my wife daily: evening conversation, date, English help, wash dishes
- Invest in kids daily: help at bedtime, assist daughter with school work, walk dog with son

Recreation:

- Keep up with US college and pro sports with friends or family
- Travel, sightsee, and explore occasionally
- Escape through fun movies, TV shows, books

Body:

- Wake up 6:30 a.m., bedtime routine 10:00 p.m.
- Exercise early every morning
- Go to bed slightly hungry in evenings—no food after 8:00 p.m.
- Stretch every morning

JONATHAN'S RULE
(in his 30s, married no kids, engineer)

Sleep 10:00 p.m. – 5:50 a.m. daily

Read Bible in mornings 4 – 5x a week

Pause 5 minutes to reflect with God 2x a day

Church weekly

Bike to work 4 – 5x a week

Soccer weekly

Small group weekly

Call Dad 5x a week

Date night weekly

Cook dinner 4x a week

Give 15 percent of income away monthly

Camping yearly (1 week)

Retreat 2x a year

Visit wife's family in Colombia yearly

ROB'S RULE
(artist in his 50s)

• *As I can,* I begin each morning by thanking God for all that will happen in the day ahead. Anticipate goodness and the Lord's love in all that will take place.

• *As I can,* I begin each day with 20 minutes of silent prayer.

• *As I can,* practice reading a short passage of Scripture as a *lectio divina* each day—a time of slow spiritual reading that has as its purpose the conversion of my heart more than the accumulation of knowledge.

• *As I can,* I will meet with a "soul friend" monthly to discuss with each other where I have struggled and where I have found encouragement from God in relation to these practices.

• *As I can,* I will meet regularly with a small group of people who know and share my deepest desires for relationship with God.

• *As I can,* I will live a simple and uncluttered life. I will enjoy time for hospitality with people I meet in my day, especially God. Invite others into my life, my home, my journey.

• *As I can,* I will find a regular outlet through which to offer my time, money, and labor for the sake of others.

• *As I can,* I plan dedicated times for spiritual retreat throughout the year—a day, a weekend, or a week away in silence with God.

MICHELLE'S RULE (married with a young child, pastor)

	Spiritual/Leisure	Mental/Emotional	Relational	Physical	Domestic/Financial	Vocational/Missional
Daily	-Morning prayer -Journal	-Read before bed (only one book at a time)	-Read with son	-Brush twice a day -Floss once a day -Water morning/each meal -5 servings veggies -24 grams of fiber -Vitamins -7–8 hours sleep	-9:00-10:00 p.m. set aside for home management, reading, and day close	
Weekly	-Sabbath (pray and play)		-Couples meeting [Fri] -Date night [Fri] -Call parents	-Work out three to five times a week -Personal grooming time	-Plan meals [Mon] -Laundry [Mon] -Budget [Mon] -Go through mail/scan [Mon]	-Work retreat [Thurs/Fri] -Plan for week ahead [Fri]
Monthly		-Visit friend	-Date with babysitting -Meaningful interactions with mentors, peers -Hang with colleague		-Tithe -Submit reimbursements	
Quarterly			-Go to hair salon			-Offsite work retreat
Biannually				-Dental cleaning		
Annually	-Monastery retreat -Revise rule of life		-Celebrate anniversary	-OB/GYN visit		-Do mission as a family -Continuing education

ACKNOWLEDGMENTS

The eighteenth-century historian Edward Gibbon began his first book with the words, "Unprovided with original learning, unformed in the habits of thinking, unskilled in the arts of composition, I resolved to write a book." I identify with his words and I am keenly aware that this book would have never come to fruition without the support, ideas, and inspiration of many other people.

Thank you, Leighton, for inviting me on the pilgrimage to Ireland, the journey that sowed the seeds of this book and for encouraging me to write and trust my voice even when I didn't.

Danae Yankoski, your agreeing to collaborate with me early on inspired me to let go of the edge of the riverbank and start to swim.

Jacob Buurma, your love for words helped me find the right ones. Sarah Tsang, your keen observations moved me to reflect more deeply on life with God.

Jade Holownia, I am indebted to you for your levelheaded "feedforward" on my preaching and writing.

Thank you, Pete and Geri Scazzero, for blazing the trail for my contemplative journey.

Mark Buchanan, your grace and spirit fill my sails.

Gordon Smith, you've been like a tough, sage Japanese-sensei. *Arigato Gozaimasu.*

Peter Mitham, your precision brings clarity to me.

I am grateful to Rob Des Cotes, Alvin Ung, Darrell Johnson, Wayman and Penny Crosby, Dan Matheson, Lee Kosa, Sam Rima, Elizabeth Archer-Klein, Chris Woodhull, Eric Taylor, Edie Dwan,

Allison Barfoot, James Peterson, Mim Wickett, Susan Phillips, Bruce Hindmarsh, James Houston, Paul Stevens, Charles Ringma, Lyle Dorsett, Jeff Reimer, Anne-Marie Ellithorpe, Suzy Welch, MaryKate Morse, and Scott Gibson for stimulating or responding to ideas in the book.

Thank you to the Shiggies: Michelle Sanchez, Jonathan Mikes, Stephen Tan, Josh Moody, Joelle Hassler, Chris Kim, Jacob Buurma, and Wendy Der for living this stuff with me year in, year out.

I am indebted to Stephen and Gail Cheung, Marian de Gier (the artist who designed the original trellis for the book), Shirley Harness, Jonathan Helmus, David Lee and Grace Kim, Ken Mair, Brittany Pousett, Jennifer Seo, Jessica Toon, Sarah Tsang, Victor Wong, Richard Weiland, and Gil and June Yeung who tested this material in our rule of life small group.

Thank you to Sue Rima, my assistant, for all the ways you've supported this book vision. Edlyn, I appreciate your being available to move project details forward.

Thank you to pastoral and support staff, board, and the Tenth community—there are too many of you to mention by name.

Ryan Pazdur, Andrew Rogers, and Greg Clouse, it's been a pleasure to work with you and the Zondervan team. You've guided me with such professionalism and care, and you made the right-sizing of the book far less painful than I feared!

Thank you, Mom and Dad, for your constant love, support, and prayers. Rie, I am grateful that you continue to offer your younger brother your not-so-common common sense. Tetsuro, bro, your candor and creativity are such gifts to me. My younger sisters, Setsu and Hana, I love the ways you keep our family close and real.

Ken Nixon, my volunteer assistant, you've been a loyal friend and endlessly generous.

I am thankful to my in-laws, the Otsuka family, for opening your heart and home in Osaka for me to write in the wee morning hours while I've been jet-lagged.

Thank you, of course, Sakiko, for being the love of my life and for your belief, perspective, and support for this vision! Joey, I see

God in you. As you grow up, I pray you would know God in your everything.

Thank you most of all to God, who through this book and throughout my days causes my heart to swell in wonder: *How can you be so loving and generous to someone like me? You know what I'm like . . .*

> Not to us, LORD, not to us
> but to your name be the glory,
> because of your love and faithfulness.
> *Psalm 115:1*

NOTES

CHAPTER 1: MONKS, SAMURAI, AND THE CHRISTIAN LIFE

1. George G. Hunter, *The Celtic Way of Evangelism: How Christianity Can Reach the West ... Again* (Nashville: Abingdon, 2000), 28. They were also deeply committed to mission. Saint Patrick helped plant some seven hundred churches; commissioned thousands of priests, monks, and nuns; and played a major role in Ireland becoming a Christian nation. See Anonymous, *Annals of the Four Masters* (Dublin, Ireland: School of Celtic Studies, 1636).

2. Ian Bradley, *Colonies of Heaven: Celtic Christian Communities* (Kelowna, BC: Northstone, 2000), 11.

3. Herbert B. Workman, *The Evolution of the Monastic Ideal* (Boston: Beacon, 1962), 139–40.

4. I am paraphrasing the words of Tim Hughes's worship song "Everything," on the album *Holding Nothing Back* (Sparrow/Survivor, 2007).

CHAPTER 2: CREATING A SPIRITUAL ECOSYSTEM

1. For a further discussion on the trellis see Peter Scazzero, *Emotionally Healthy Spirituality* (Nashville: Thomas Nelson, 2001); and David Steindl Rast, *Music of Silence* (Berkeley, CA: Ulysses, 1995).

234 GOD IN MY EVERYTHING

2. Dallas Willard, *The Great Omission: Reclaiming Jesus' Essential Teachings on Discipleship* (San Francisco: HarperSanFrancisco, 2006), 80.

3. Both Paul and Peter emphasize that we are called to display the fruit of Jesus' character in our lives: love, joy, kindness, self-control, patience, and so on. Both Paul and Peter, moreover, affirm the role of God's grace in this process (Galatians 5:22–23; 2 Peter 1:5–7), but while Paul emphasizes the role of the Holy Spirit, Peter calls us to "make every effort" to add to our faith qualities like goodness, self-control, love, and so on. These writers of Scripture are not contradicting each other; rather, they recognize the role that both God and we play in our growth. Paul simply emphasizes God's role and Peter our role.

4. 1 Corinthians 9:25.

5. Dallas Willard and John Ortberg use this image as well. See Dallas Willard, *The Divine Conspiracy* (San Francisco: HarperSanFrancisco, 1998), 313–39; and John Ortberg, *The Life You've Always Wanted* (Grand Rapids: Zondervan, 1997), ch. 3.

6. As a result, Dallas Willard has pointed out that training through spiritual disciplines enables us to do what we cannot now do by direct effort. It's like weight training, in which a rhythm of deliberate practice over time will give us power to bench press something in the future that we cannot lift now.

7. I am drawing on Jesuit terminology here.

8. Thomas Merton, *New Seeds of Contemplation* (New York: New Directions, 1961), 19.

9. Evelyn Underhill, *The Spiritual Life* (Harrisburg, PA: Morehouse, 1955), 93–94.

10. Patrick Henry, ed., *Benedict's Dharma* (New York: Riverhead, 2001), 2, 19.

11. Ronald Rolheiser, *Forgotten Among the Lilies* (Toronto: Doubleday, 2005), 116.

12. Matthew 14:13–14.

13. Thomas R. Kelly, *A Testament of Devotion* (San Francisco: HarperSanFrancisco, 1941), 93.

CHAPTER 3: A RULE THAT BENDS

1. Thomas Moore cited in James White, *Serious Times: Making Your Life Count in an Urgent Day* (Downers Grove, IL: InterVarsity Press, 2004), 90.

2. See Daniel 5:14.

3. Kathleen Norris, *Acedia and Me: A Marriage, Monks, and A Writer's Life* (New York: Riverhead, 2008), 187.

4. I thank Jim White for helping to create this image for me.

5. John F. Mogabgab, "The Vineyard, Editor's Introduction," *Weavings* 16, no. 5 (September/October 2001): 2–3.

6. Jim Loehr and Tony Schwartz, *The Power of Full Engagement: Managing Energy, Not Time, Is the Key to High Performance and Personal Renewal* (New York: Free Press, 2003), 3–5.

7. Michelle Sanchez, who is part of a mentoring group I lead, in an unpublished paper while a student at Gordon-Conwell Theological Seminary made the observation that the gentle balance and flexibility that characterize Benedict's rule may well be why it has proved to be more enduring and influential than any other.

8. Alan Deutschmann, *Change or Die* (New York: HarperCollins, 2007), 1–5.

9. Hebrews 3:12–13.

CHAPTER 4: SABBATH: OASIS FOR BODY AND SOUL

1. Timothy Fry, ed., *The Rule of St. Benedict in English* (Collegeville, MN: Liturgical Press, 1981), chs. 11–12.

2. Thomas Merton, *Conjectures of a Guilty Bystander* (Garden City, NY: Doubleday, 1966), 73.

3. Wayne Muller, *Sabbath: Restoring the Sacred Rhythm of Rest* (New York: Bantam, 1999), 69.

4. Eugene H. Peterson, "The Pastor's Sabbath," *Leadership* 55 (Spring 1985): 82.

5. Why one day in seven? Marva Dawn, in *Keeping the Sabbath Wholly: Ceasing, Resting, Embracing, Feasting* (Grand Rapids: Eerdmans, 1989), 69, cites Juan-Carlos Lerman at the University of Arizona, whose research shows that we have a biological need for rest every seventh day. According to his theory, failing to rest after six days of steady work will lead to insomnia, or sleepiness, hormonal imbalances, fatigue, irritability, organ stress, and other increasingly serious physical and mental symptoms. Not taking one day in seven as a Sabbath also makes people more vulnerable to addiction.

6. The Sabbath provides us with what Rabbi Abraham Heschel has called a "sanctuary in time." See Abraham Heschel, *The Sabbath* (New York: Farrar, Straus and Giroux, 1951).

7. Eugene Peterson, *Answering God: The Psalms as Tools for Prayer* (New York: HarperCollins, 1989), 65.

8. In Psalm 127 we are reminded that God provides for us while we sleep. The Hebrew in Psalm 127:2 can be read "He gives his beloved sleep" or "He gives to his beloved while they sleep." In Psalm 127 the psalmist encourages a person to refrain from rising early and staying up late because they are anxious about their productivity and to instead trust that God will provide for them. Based on the context, I believe the second reading is the more plausible one: he grants to his beloved *in* sleep.

9. Dawn, *Keeping the Sabbath Wholly*, 9.

10. See Mark 2:27.

11. Mark Buchanan, *The Rest of God: Restoring Your Soul by Restoring Sabbath* (Nashville: Thomas Nelson, 2006), 126.

12. James E. Loehr and Tony Schwartz, *The Power of Full Engagement: Managing Energy, Not Time, Is the Key to High Performance and Personal Renewal* (New York: Free Press, 2003), 42.

13. Matthew 11:28–29.

CHAPTER 5: PRAYER: DEEPENING YOUR FRIENDSHIP WITH GOD

1. Simon Tugwell emphasizes that prayer is a gift. See Simon Tugwell, *Prayer in Practice* (Springfield, IL: Templegate, 1974), 3–15.

2. Richard J. Foster, *Celebration of Discipline: The Path to Spiritual Growth* (San Francisco: Harper and Row, 1978), 33.

3. Gordon T. Smith, *On the Way: A Guide to Christian Spirituality* (Colorado Springs: NavPress, 2001), 71.

4. Tugwell, *Prayer in Practice*, 6.

5. Psalm 55:17.

6. Tugwell, *Prayer in Practice*, 13.

7. One way to do this is to schedule an occasional retreat.

8. C. S. Lewis, *The Screwtape Letters* (London: Collins), 25.

9. Dietrich Bonhoeffer, *Life Together* (New York: Harper and Row, 1954), 62–63.

10. Quoted in Ruth Haley Barton, *Sacred Rhythms: Arranging Our Lives for Spiritual Transformation* (Downers Grove, IL: InterVarsity Press, 2006), 62.

11. M. Basil Pennington, *Centering Prayer: Renewing an Ancient Christian Prayer Form* (New York: Doubleday, 2001), 50.

12. Psalm 46:10.

13. Recounted in James Martin, *The Jesuit Guide to (Almost) Everything: A Spirituality for Real Life* (San Francisco: HarperOne, 2010), 102.

14. I am paraphrasing Thomas Merton quoted in Martin S. Laird, *Into the Silent Land: A Guide to the Christian Practice of Contemplation* (Oxford: Oxford University Press, 2006), 53.

CHAPTER 6: NOURISHING YOUR SOUL THROUGH SACRED READING

1. See Matthew 4:4.

2. Eugene H. Peterson, *Answering God: The Psalms as Tools for Prayer* (San Francisco: HarperSanFrancisco, 1991), 24.

3. Isaiah 31:4.

4. Eugene Peterson, *Eat This Book* (Grand Rapids: Eerdmans, 2006), 1.

5. A. W. Tozer, *The Pursuit of God* (Harrisburg, PA: Christian Publications, 1982), 10.

6. *Lectio divina* employs the steps of *lectio* (Reading), *meditatio* (Meditation), *oratio* (Praying), and *contemplatio* (Contemplation). Often in practice they are not sequential, but I am using the term *lectio divina* in a more general way to describe a prayerful, meditative reading of Scripture. See Michael Casey, *Sacred Reading: The Ancient Art of Lectio Divina* (Liguori, MO: Triumph Books, 1996), 44.

7. Dietrich Bonhoeffer, *Meditating on the Word* (Cambridge, MA: Cowley, 2000), 33.

8. Peterson, *Eat This Book*, 3–4.

9. Ibid., 14–17.

10. Ibid., 17.

11. Jean Leclercq, *The Love of Learning and the Desire for God: A*

Study of Monastic Culture (New York: Fordham University Press, 1961), 15.

12. As Michael Casey notes in *Sacred Reading* (Liguori, MO: Liguori Publications, 1997).

13. Casey, *Sacred Reading*, 84.

14. Christopher Hall, "Reading Christ into the Heart: The Theological Foundations of *Lectio Divina*," in *Life in the Spirit: Spiritual Formation in Theological Perspective*, eds. Jeffrey P. Greenman and George Kalantzis (Downers Grove, IL: IVP Academic, 2010), 155–56.

15. *The Spiritual Exercises of Saint Ignatius of Loyola*, trans. Elder Mullan (Grand Rapids: Christian Classics Ethereal Library, 1991), 214–64.

16. William of Saint Thierry (d. 1148), *The Golden Epistle: A Letter to the Brethren at Mont Dieu* 1.120–24, trans. Theodore Berkeley, in *The Works of William of St. Thierry*, Cistercian Fathers 12 (Spencer, MA: Cistercian Publications, 1971), 51–52.

17. Leclercq, *Love of Learning*, 13–17.

CHAPTER 7: FRIENDSHIP: COMPANIONS FOR THE JOURNEY

1. Hal Niedzviecki, "Facebook in a Crowd," *New York Times*, accessed February 5, 2010, http://www.nytimes.com/2008/10/26/magazine/26lives-t.html.

2. William Deresiewicz, "Faux Friendship," *Chronicle of Higher Education*, accessed February 23, 2012, http://chronicle.com/article/Faux-Friendship/49308/.

3. Robert D. Putnam, *Bowling Alone: The Collapse and Revival of American Community* (New York: Simon and Schuster, 2000), 39.

4. Mary Bray Pipher, *Another Country: Navigating the Emotional Terrain of Our Elders* (New York: Riverhead, 1999), 170.

5.   Joshua Wolf Shenk, "What Makes Us Happy?" *Atlantic*, June, 2006, accessed February 10, 2010, http://www.theatlantic.com/magazine/archive/2009/06/what-makes-us-happy/7439/.

6.   Genesis 1:31.

7.   See Genesis 2:18.

8.   As my friend Darrell Johnson likes to say.

9.   Paul J. Wadell, *Friendships and the Moral Life* (Notre Dame, IN: University of Notre Dame Press, 1989), 101.

10.   1 Samuel 20:14–15.

11.   Aelred of Rievaulx. *Spiritual Friendship*, trans. Mary Eugenia Laker, SSND (Kalamazoo, MI: Cistercian, 1977), cited in Paul J. Wadell, *Becoming Friends: Worship, Justice, and the Practice of Christian Friendship* (Grand Rapids: Brazos, 2002), 113.

12.   Wadell, *Becoming Friends*, 116.

13.   Richard Rohr and Joseph Martos, *From Wild Man to Wise Man: Reflections on Male Spirituality* (Cincinnati: St. Anthony Messenger Press, 2005), 172.

14.   John O'Donohue, *Anam Cara: A Book of Celtic Wisdom* (New York: HarperCollins, 1998), 13.

15.   Aelred of Rievaulx, *Spiritual Friendship*, 3.83 (114).

16.   Ibid.

17.   I could not find the source. I believe it was from one of Merton's unpublished talks.

18.   Aelred, *Spiritual Friendship*, 3.84 (113).

19.   Aelred, *Spiritual Friendship*, 3.40 (100).

20.   Aelred, *Spiritual Friendship*, 2.11 (72).

21.   O'Donohue, *Anam Cara*, 25.

22.   Wadell, *Becoming Friends*, 107.

23. Deresiewicz, "Faux Friendship."

24. Aelred, op. cit., Book 1:1, 51.

25. Deresiewicz, "Faux Friendship."

26. John 15:15.

CHAPTER 8: SEX AND SPIRITUALITY

1. Ronald Rolheiser, *The Holy Longing: The Search for a Christian Spirituality* (New York: Doubleday, 1999), 196. The *Anchor Bible Dictionary* notes there is a synthesis between *agape* and *eros*: "If ecstasy is at the center of the idea of *eros*, then surely there is no true *agape* without it" (David Noel Freedman, ed., *Anchor Bible Dictionary, Volume 4: K-N* (New York: Doubleday, 1992), 385. In the Song of Solomon the Hebrew words for love: *ahava* (loyal love), *raya* (friendship), and *dodim* (erotic love) are also weaved together and have overlapping meanings.

2. Rolheiser, *The Holy Longing*, 193.

3. Gordon Neufeld and Gabor Mate, *Hold On to Your Kids: Why Parents Need to Matter More Than Peers* (New York: Ballantine, 2005), 159.

4. The word that Paul uses for sexual immorality is the Greek word *porneia* which refers to sex outside of marriage: prostitution, adultery, and premarital sex (also see Galatians 5:19; 1 Thessalonians 4:3).

5. In *The Brain That Changes Itself*, Dr. Norman Doidge, MD describes how pornography addiction is like a drug addiction. For addicts, moderation is impossible and so they must avoid the activity, whatever it is, completely. Cocaine, like non-drug addictions such as running, makes the pleasure-giving neurotransmitter dopamine more active in the brain. Dopamine is a "reward transmitter," and when we accomplish something our brain releases it. By hijacking our dopamine system, addictive substances give us pleasure without our having to work

for it. Doidge equates porn with cocaine in terms of its addictive nature. Viewing porn releases the same dopamine that is released in sexual excitement and hence has the same addictive power. "Porn often delivers an addiction, tolerance, and an eventual decrease in pleasure." The neuroscience of it all is that the map of our brain is changed forever and a person needs increasing amounts of it or more violent images to remain satisfied. Norman Doidge, *The Brain That Changes Itself: The Frontiers of Brain Science* (London: Penguin, 2007), 102–9.

6. Lauren F. Winner, *Real Sex: The Naked Truth about Chastity* (Grand Rapids: Brazos, 2005), 106–7.

7. See http://davecarder.com/.

8. Shirley P. Glass and Jean Coppock Staeheli. *Not "Just Friends": Rebuilding Trust and Recovering Your Sanity after Infidelity* (New York: Free Press, 2003), 25–26.

9. Naomi Wolf, "Naomi Wolf on Why Porn Turns Men Off the Real Thing," *New York Magazine,* accessed March 28, 2010, http://nymag.com/nymetro/news/trends/n_9437/.

10. Matthew 5:29–30.

11. Attributed to G. K. Chesterton.

12. James Martin, *The Jesuit Guide to (Almost) Everything: A Spirituality for Real Life* (San Francisco: HarperOne, 2010), 222.

13. See John Mordechai Gottman and Nan Silver, *Why Marriages Succeed or Fail: What You Can Learn from the Breakthrough Research to Make Your Marriage Last* (New York: Simon and Schuster, 1994).

14. Kathleen Norris, *The Cloister Walk* (New York: Riverhead, 1996), 120.

15. Ibid., 120–23.

16. Richard J. Foster, *Money, Sex, and Power: The Challenge of the Disciplined Life* (San Francisco: Harper and Row, 1985), 6.

17. Ronald Rolheiser, *Forgotten Among the Lilies: Learning to Live Beyond Our Fears* (New York: Doubleday, 2005), 88.

CHAPTER 9: FAMILY TIES

1. My interview with Father Mark Dumont, August, 2011.

2. Ronald Rolheiser, *Forgotten Among the Lilies: Learning to Live Beyond Our Fears* (New York: Doubleday, 2005), 314–15.

3. I am paraphrasing Gary Thomas. See Gary L. Thomas, *Sacred Marriage* (Grand Rapids: Zondervan, 2000), 13.

4. Neil MacQueen, "The Life Benefits of Regular Church Attendance," *The Sunday Software*, accessed October 15, 2011, http://www.sundaysoftware.com/stats.htm.

5. Paraphrased from Stephen Covey, *First Things First* (New York: Free Press, 1994), 88.

6. Timothy Fry, ed., *The Rule of St. Benedict in English* (Collegeville, MN: Liturgical Press, 1981), 73.

7. James Martin, *The Jesuit Guide to (Almost) Everything: A Spirituality for Real Life* (San Francisco: HarperOne, 2010), 245.

8. Thomas W. Ogletree, *Hospitality to the Stranger* (Philadelphia: Fortress, 1985), 46.

9. RB 48, 38: Fry, ed., *Rule of St. Benedict*, 69, 60.

10. "Americans Watching More TV Than Ever; Web and Mobile Video Up Too," *NielsenWire*, May 20, 2009, accessed April 22, 2012, http://blog.nielsen.com/nielsenwire/online_mobile/americans-watching-more-tv-than-ever/.

11. RB 48: Fry, ed., *Rule of St. Benedict*, 69.

12. A New York University Child Study Center reported that financially privileged adolescents (defined as coming from households with incomes from $75,000 to $160,000) are showing growing rates of school failure, depression, anxiety, and substance

use. In the last thirty years, adolescent suicide in this group has doubled. The report noted affluent teenagers had great freedom to learn and had a wide range of opportunities for recreation and entertainment, but these teens often showed signs of apathy, laziness, or failure to commit to and achieve goals, to overindulgence and attitudes of entitlement. "The Parent Letter," May 2007, accessed January 11, 2011, http://www.aboutourkids.org/files/articles/english_parent_letter_may_07.pdf.

13. Mark 8:31–35.

CHAPTER 10: EAT, SLEEP, SWIM

1. I am paraphrasing John Cassian's ideas; see *John Cassian: Conferences*, trans. Colm Luibheid (Mahwah, NJ: Paulist Press, 1985), 76–80.

2. For example, through harsh ascetical practices, John Chrysostom ruined his digestive system and did not lie down to sleep for two years. Simeon Stylites achieved fame by living on top of a pillar for thirty-seven years near Aleppo in Syria.

3. 1 Corinthians 6:19–20.

4. For people who are physically disabled in some way, the hope of resurrection—in which our whole selves, including our bodies, will be redeemed—is especially encouraging.

5. Dallas Willard, *The Divine Conspiracy* (San Francisco: HarperSanFrancisco, 1998), 86.

6. I first began thinking about Elijah as a story in which Gods displays his concern for our whole person when Leighton Ford preached on God's restoration of Elijah at Amsterdam 86.

7. See RB 8.1: Timothy Fry, ed., *The Rule of St. Benedict in English* (Collegeville, MN: Liturgical Press, 1981), 38.

8. William C. Dement, *The Promise of Sleep* (New York: Dell, 2000), 263.

9. Dorothy C. Bass, *Receiving the Day* (San Francisco: Jossey-Bass, 2001), 33.

10. Quoted in Tim Loerh and Tony Schwartz, *The Power of Full Engagement* (New York: Free Press, 2003), 61.

11. The Order of Saint Benedict, *The Rule of Benedict, English*, 2003, http://www.osb.org/rb/text/rbemjo2.html (accessed February 16, 2011).

12. Matthew 6:31.

13. R. Paul Stevens and Alvin Ung, *Taking Your Soul to Work: Overcoming the Nine Deadly Sins of the Workplace* (Grand Rapids: Eerdmans, 2010), 34.

14. D. Martin Lloyd-Jones, *Studies in the Sermon on the Mount* (Grand Rapids: Eerdmans, 1960), 2:38. He said, "Fasting, if we conceive of it truly, must not ... be confined to the question of food and drink; fasting should really be made to include abstinence from anything which is legitimate in and of itself for the sake of some special spiritual purpose. There are many bodily functions which are right and normal and perfectly legitimate, but which for special peculiar reasons in certain circumstances should be controlled. That is fasting."

15. Richard J. Foster, *Celebration of Discipline: The Path to Spiritual Growth* (San Francisco: Harper and Row, 1978), 66.

16. 1 Timothy 4:8.

17. Debra K. Farrington, *Living Faith Day By Day* (New York: Perigee, 2000), 180.

18. Gerald G. May, *Addiction and Grace: Love and Spirituality in the Healing of Addictions* (San Francisco: HarperSanFrancisco, 1988), 21–27.

19. Kathleen Norris, *The Quotidian Mysteries: Laundry, Liturgy and "Women's Work"* (Mahwah, NJ: Paulist Press, 1998), cited in Bass, *Receiving*, 32.

20. Parker J. Palmer, *Let Your Life Speak: Listening to the Voice of Your Vocation* (San Francisco: Jossey-Bass, 2001), 30.

CHAPTER 11: PLAY LIKE A CHILD

1. The *Washington Post* was conducting a hidden-camera experiment to see if people would stop to listen to something truly beautiful, or if they would simply hurry past.

2. Ronald Rolheiser, *The Holy Longing: The Search for a Christian Spirituality* (New York: Doubleday, 1999), 60–61.

3. Ibid., 67.

4. Ronald Rolheiser, *Forgotten Among the Lilies: Learning to Live Beyond Our Fears* (New York: Doubleday, 2005), 115.

5. Ecclesiastes 3:4.

6. Zechariah 8:5.

7. See Genesis 1:31.

8. Job 38:4, 7 (emphasis added).

9. A wedding celebration in Jesus' day typically lasted two to three days and could last up to a week.

10. Matthew 11:19.

11. Mark 10:13–16; Luke 18:15–17.

12. Gerard Manley Hopkins, "As Kingfishers Catch Fire," in *Poems of Gerard Manley Hopkins* (London: Humphrey Milford, 1918).

13. In fact, if some *benefit* of play becomes more important than play itself, it is arguable that we are no longer playing. Stuart Brown, MD with Christopher Vaughan, *Play: How It Shapes the Brain, Opens the Imagination, and Invigorates the Soul* (New York: Penguin, 2009), 17.

14. Os Guinness, *The Call: Finding and Fulfilling the Central Purpose of Your Life* (Nashville: Thomas Nelson, 1998), 190.

15. For others with a different temperament, competitive sailing or competitive sport may be an ideal form of play.

16. Brown with Vaughan, *Play*, 59–60.

17. Ibid., 33–34.

18. C. S. Lewis, *Surprised by Joy: The Shape of My Early Life* (London: Collins, 1955), 7–8.

19. Brown with Vaughan, *Play*, 177.

20. William A. Barry and William J. Connolly, *The Practice of Spiritual Direction* (New York: HarperCollins, 1986), 49.

21. Ibid., 50.

22. I am drawing this insight from William A. Barry, *A Friendship Like No Other: Experiencing God's Amazing Grace* (Chicago: Loyola University Press, 2008), 33–34.

CHAPTER 12: MONEY: MASTER OR SERVANT?

1. Matthew 6:24.

2. Os Guinness, *The Call: Finding and Fulfilling the Central Purpose of Your Life* (Nashville: Thomas Nelson, 1998), 132.

3. This is a paraphrase. "There are three conversions necessary in the Christian life: the conversion of the heart, [the conversion of] the mind, and [the conversion of] the purse." From Richard J. Foster, *Money, Sex, and Power: The Challenge of the Disciplined Life* (San Francisco: Harper and Row, 1985), 19.

4. I am paraphrasing Pastor Victor Shepherd.

5. 1 Timothy 6:6.

6. Philippians 4:11–13.

7. At which point they were basically as satisfied with their lives as a sample of university students drawn from about fifty nations.

8. Bill McKibben, *Deep Economy: The Wealth of Communities and the Durable Future* (New York: Times Books, 2007), 41–42.

9. Matthew 6:21.

10. Dave Denison, "Watching the Rich Give," *New York Times Magazine*, March 9, 2008, accessed July 10, 2010, http://www.nytimes.com/2008/03/09/magazine/09wwlnidealab-t.html.

11. There were three tithes in Israel. One of them was given every third year, so these people were giving 23 percent of their income annually. While God's people were living in exile, they faced heavy taxation from the Persians.

12. 1 Corinthians 16:2.

13. To read more about proportionate giving, see Ronald Sider's *Rich Christians in an Age of Hunger* (Nashville: Thomas Nelson, 2005).

14. Wesley was also single for much of his life and never had any children of his own. His rule likely would have been modified in some way if he had been supporting a larger family. See Richard J. Foster, *Freedom of Simplicity* (New York: HarperCollins, 1981), 131.

15. Ibid., 145.

16. James Martin, *The Jesuit Guide to (Almost) Everything: A Spirituality for Real Life* (San Francisco: HarperOne, 2010), 179.

17. John Chrysostom, *On Wealth and Poverty* (New York: St. Vladimir's Seminary Press, 1999), 46–47.

CHAPTER 13: THANK GOD IT'S MONDAY

1. Genesis 2:9.

2. James Martin, *The Jesuit Guide to (Almost) Everything* (San Francisco: HarperOne, 2010), 372.

3. Ibid., 372.

4. John 5:17.

5. John 16:8.

6. Joan Chittister, *Wisdom Distilled from the Daily* (San Francisco: HarperSanFrancisco, 1990), 84.

7. 1 Corinthians 3:6.

8. Dallas Willard, *The Divine Conspiracy* (San Francisco: HarperSanFrancisco, 1998), 285.

9. Mayeul de Dreuille, *The Rule of Saint Benedict: A Commentary in Light of World Ascetic Traditions* (New York: Newman Press, 2000), 236.

10. 1 Thessalonians 5:17.

11. Columba Stewart, *Cassian the Monk* (New York: Oxford University Press, 1998), 113. I am drawing on the work of Michelle Sanchez's unpublished paper at Gordon-Conwell Theological Seminary.

12. Nigel Thrift, "Vivo Voco: Ringing the Changes in the Historical Geography of Time Consciousness," in Michael Dunlop Young and Tom Schuller, *The Rhythms of Society* (New York: Taylor and Francis, 1988), 75.

13. Paul Stevens and Alvin Ung, *Taking Your Soul to Work* (Grand Rapids: Eerdmans, 2010), 124.

14. Jean François-Millet, *The Angelus*, ca. 1857–59, oil on canvas, 55.5 x 66 cm, the Musée d'Orsay, Paris.

15. Colossians 3:23.

16. Wikipedia, "Brother Lawrence," accessed July 17, 2011, http://en.wikipedia.org/wiki/Brother_Lawrence.

17. In Benedict's day, though slavery was commonplace, the monasteries refused to use slaves. Benedict would not allow the monastery to "benefit" from unjust labor. In the monasteries, as we've noted, everyone from the former slave to a person of

royal ancestry participated in manual labor. The children of the nobles worked side by side with the children of serfs. No one class of people bore a disproportionate burden.

18. Luke 22:42.

19. Dennis L. Okholm, *Monk Habits for Everyday People: Benedictine Spirituality for Protestants* (Grand Rapids: Brazos, 2007), 92.

20. RB: 1. Timothy Fry, ed., *The Rule of St. Benedict in English* (Collegeville, MN: Liturgical Press, 1981), 20–21.

21. Parker Palmer, *Let Your Life Speak* (San Francisco: Jossey-Bass, 2000), 45–46.

22. Fry, ed. *Rule of St. Benedict*, 20–21.

CHAPTER 14: SENDING A RIPPLE THROUGH ETERNITY

1. Matthew 25:34–39.

2. Romans 5:5.

3. Jeffery Jones, "Christian Students More Willing to Help Katrina Victims," *Preaching Today*, accessed March 2, 2012, http://www. preachingtoday.com/illustrations/2006/march/4032706.html.

4. Rikk Watts, Reframe course lecture given at Tenth Church, April 12–June 14, 2011, Vancouver, BC.

5. Phillip E. Johnson, *Darwin on Trial* (Downers Grove, IL: InterVarsity Press, 1991), 144.

6. Thomas Cahill, *How the Irish Saved Civilization* (New York: Doubleday, 1995), 148.

7. Elizabeth Skoglund, *Amma: The Life and Words of Amy Carmichael* (Grand Rapids: Baker, 1999), 72–73.

8. Of course, theologians differ as to how literally we are to interpret that.

9. Richard Stearns, *The Hole in Our Gospel* (Nashville: Thomas Nelson, 2009), 14.

10. I thank my former professor Haddon Robinson for this insight from the Luke 10 story of Mary and Martha.

11. Luke 5:16.

12. Luke 6:12–16.

13. John 14:10.

14. Scott A. Bessenecker, ed., *Living Mission: The Vision and Voices of New Friars* (Downers Grove, IL: InterVarsity Press, 2010), 28.

15. Ibid., 108.

16. Mike Yankoski and Danae Yankoski, *Zealous Love* (Grand Rapids: Zondervan), 27–29.

17. From a sermon given by Darrell Johnson, Tenth Avenue Alliance Church, June 14, 2009.

18. Though the *Vancouver Sun* article didn't explicitly mention this, he has entered into a friendship with Christ.

19. N. T. Wright, *Surprised by Hope* (New York: HarperOne, 2007), 193.

20. Ibid., 208.

CHAPTER 15: SHARING THE PRESENCE

1. Gordon Smith, *Beginning Well: Christian Conversion and Authentic Transformation* (Downers Grove, IL: InterVarsity Press, 2001), 89.

2. John 15:20.

3. Bryant L. Myers, *Walking with the Poor* (Maryknoll, NY: Orbis, 1999), 212–14.

4. 1 Peter 2:12.

5.   Matthew 5:16.

6.   John 10:38.

7.   Romans 10:14, my paraphrase.

8.   Elton Trueblood, *Confronting Christ* (Waco, TX: Word, 1960), 12.

Share Your Thoughts

With the Author: Your comments will be forwarded to the author when you send them to *zauthor@zondervan.com*.

With Zondervan: Submit your review of this book by writing to *zreview@zondervan.com*.

Free Online Resources at
www.zondervan.com

Zondervan AuthorTracker: Be notified whenever your favorite authors publish new books, go on tour, or post an update about what's happening in their lives at www.zondervan.com/authortracker.

Daily Bible Verses and Devotions: Enrich your life with daily Bible verses or devotions that help you start every morning focused on God. Visit www.zondervan.com/newsletters.

Free Email Publications: Sign up for newsletters on Christian living, academic resources, church ministry, fiction, children's resources, and more. Visit www.zondervan.com/newsletters.

Zondervan Bible Search: Find and compare Bible passages in a variety of translations at www.zondervanbiblesearch.com.

Other Benefits: Register yourself to receive online benefits like coupons and special offers, or to participate in research.